CONTENTS

1987 AT A GLANCE

JANUARY 1.   People in the United States began to celebrate 1987 as the Year of the Reader—a time to stress the importance of reading. National, state, and local projects were organized across the country to encourage people to read more and to make reading a more valued activity.

JANUARY 16.   In China, Hu Yaobang was forced to resign as Communist Party leader, the most important political office in the country. He had held the post since 1981. Premier Zhao Ziyang was appointed to replace him.

FEBRUARY 24.   Astronomers at an observatory in the mountains of Chile announced that they had discovered a huge supernova, or exploding star. The supernova was about 160,000 light years from Earth. (In other words, the light reaching Earth was generated by an explosion that occurred 160,000 years ago. A light year is the distance light travels in one year—about 6 trillion miles.) It was the closest and brightest supernova to be seen since 1604. By observing it, astronomers expect to learn a great deal about these explosions, their origins, and their role in the evolution of the universe.

MARCH 31.   Researchers reported the discovery of the first rock painting of an Ice Age animal to be found outside Europe. The painting was discovered in Queensland, Australia. It shows a diprotodon, a rhinoceros-sized marsupial that became extinct about 6,000 years ago. The rock painting seems to show ropes around the diprotodon—which suggests that the animal may have been domesticated.

MAY 17.   The U.S.S. *Stark,* a Navy frigate on patrol in the Persian Gulf, was struck by missiles fired by an Iraqi warplane. Thirty-seven American sailors were killed in the attack, which Iraq said was accidental. It was the first serious attack on American forces in the Persian Gulf since the start of the war between Iran and Iraq in 1980.

MAY 24.   Fireworks, a parade of ships, a 50-gun salute, and other festivities marked the 50th anniversary of the Golden Gate Bridge. The bridge, which spans San Francisco Bay, was considered an engineering marvel when it opened in 1937 and is still famous for its beauty. During the anniversary celebrations, some 250,000 people crowded onto it—so many that their weight briefly flattened the normal arch of the bridge deck.

JUNE 26.   Justice Lewis F. Powell, Jr., retired from the U.S. Supreme Court. A member of the Court since 1971, Powell was considered a moderate in his views. He was the "swing vote" on many recent Court decisions, providing the critical fifth vote needed for a majority. (On July 1, President Ronald Reagan nominated Judge Robert H. Bork to succeed Powell. On October 23, the Senate voted not to confirm Bork because of his strongly conservative interpretations of the Constitution.)

JULY 25.   U.S. Secretary of Commerce Malcolm Baldrige died in a horseback riding accident. He had been a member of President Ronald Reagan's Cabinet since 1981. (On August 10, C. William Verity, Jr., was named to succeed Baldrige.)

JULY 26.   A French underwater expedition retrieved dishes from the wreckage of the Titanic—the first objects ever recovered from the luxury ocean liner that hit an iceberg and sank on its maiden voyage in 1912. The wreckage lies on the floor of the Atlantic Ocean, several hundred miles south of Newfoundland. (By the time the French team ended their 46-day project, they had retrieved about 300 artifacts, including more dishes, a pair of gold spectacles, a silver ladle, and some money and jewels. Many people, however, had objected to the expedition. They had urged that the ship remain untouched and be left as a memorial to those who had died in the disaster.)

JULY 31.   In Mecca, Saudi Arabia, more than 400 people died when fighting broke out between Saudi riot police and Iranian Muslims who were staging a political demonstration. Mecca is Islam's holiest city, and hundreds of thousands of Muslim pilgrims from many countries had gathered there on the eve of the annual pilgrimage, or *hajj,* which marks the high point of the Islamic year. The Saudi government doesn't allow political demonstrations in Mecca during the *hajj,* but the Iranians ignored the ban.

AUGUST 15. The Great Basin National Park, in eastern Nevada, was dedicated as the 49th national park in the United States. Covering 77,109 acres of deserts and mountains, it was the first new national park in the 48 contiguous states in fifteen years. The park includes Wheeler Peak (which has the southernmost glacier in the United States) and Lehman Caves (which is the largest limestone cavern in the West).

SEPTEMBER 14. Elizabeth Hanford Dole announced that she would resign as U.S. Secretary of Transportation. (On October 8, James H. Burnley IV was named to succeed Dole.)

SEPTEMBER 16. Twenty-four nations, including the United States and Canada, signed a treaty designed to protect the ozone layer in the Earth's atmosphere. Ozone, a form of oxygen, absorbs much of the sun's harmful ultraviolet radiation. For many years, scientists have warned that the ozone shield was being destroyed by chlorofluorocarbons (CFC's). These industrial chemicals are used in refrigerants, solvents, foam insulation, and as propellants in aerosol sprays. And recently, scientists discovered severe thinning of the ozone layer over the Antarctic. Under the terms of the treaty, CFC production would be reduced 50 percent by 1999. The treaty marked the first time that the world's nations had agreed to cooperate on an environmental problem.

OCTOBER 1. A severe earthquake followed by numerous aftershocks hit the Los Angeles area. The quake, the strongest to hit the area since 1971, caused seven deaths and many injuries. Property damage was estimated at more than $200 million.

OCTOBER 15. William E. Brock announced that he would resign as U.S. Secretary of Labor. (On November 3, Ann Dore McLaughlin was named to succeed Brock.)

OCTOBER 19. The day became known as "Black Monday," as the U.S. stock market had its worst day in history. The Dow Jones industrial average—the major indicator of changes in the level of stock prices—fell 508 points. More than 604 million shares were traded. The frantic trading and plunging prices were followed by similar events on stock markets elsewhere in the world.

OCTOBER 29. President Ronald Reagan nominated Judge Douglas H. Ginsburg to the U.S. Supreme Court. (On November 7, Ginsburg withdrew as nominee, following disclosures that he had smoked marijuana in the past.)

NOVEMBER 4. It was announced that scientists had identified fossils of the largest seabird ever known. The fossils were discovered in an excavation made in 1984 in Charleston, South Carolina. They were in rock dated at about 30 million years old. The creature was a member of the extinct family *pseudodontorn* ("bony-toothed bird"). Its jaws were lined with rough, bony structures that looked somewhat like teeth. It had a wingspan of more than 18 feet (5.5 meters)—in comparison, the largest living seabird, the albatross, has a wingspan of 11 feet (3.4 meters).

NOVEMBER 5. Caspar W. Weinberger announced his resignation as U.S. Secretary of Defense. Frank C. Carlucci was named to succeed Weinberger.

NOVEMBER 11. President Ronald Reagan nominated Judge Anthony M. Kennedy to the U.S. Supreme Court. It was Reagan's third nomination to fill the seat left vacant by the resignation of Lewis F. Powell, Jr.

DECEMBER 8. At a historic summit meeting in Washington, D.C., U.S. President Ronald Reagan and Soviet leader Mikhail Gorbachev signed the first treaty reducing the size of their countries' nuclear arms. It calls for both countries to destroy within three years all their intermediate-range nuclear missiles (missiles with ranges of 300 to 3,400 miles). And it sets up a system of inspections to ensure that the missile destruction is carried out. The agreement was the product of two years of negotiations, and it still must be ratified by the U.S. Senate.

DECEMBER 29. Three Soviet cosmonauts aboard a Soyuz spacecraft returned to the Soviet Union from the Earth-orbiting space station Mir. One of the cosmonauts, Yuri Romanenko, had spent 326 days on the space station—thus setting a new space-endurance record.

ONCE UPON A FLOWER

Tulips in a garden, goldenrod by the side of the road—who would think that these common flowers are bits of living history and legend? But every flower has a story to tell. Some of the flowers that are best loved today have been favorites since early times. And over the years, they've become surrounded with lore—some fact, some fancy, but all fascinating.

BACHELOR'S BUTTON

The bright blue cornflowers that are called bachelor's buttons figure in many legends, some of them very old. The ancient Greeks recounted how Chiron, the centaur, cured an arrow wound by covering it with these flowers. Right through the 1800's, bachelor's buttons were used in some medicines. And some people believed that burning them would drive away snakes.

The flower's odd name is thought to have come from a practice that developed in Scotland long ago. There, a young man who was unsure of his girlfriend's affections would pick a cornflower and put it in his pocket. If it survived unwilted for a day, all was well, and the two were sure to be married.

CARNATION

The showy florists' carnations we're familiar with are a modern creation. For most of its history, the carnation was a smaller, simpler flower, more like its close cousin the pink. Both these flowers belong to the genus *Dianthus,* and the genus name reflects their ancient history. It was bestowed by the Greeks in the fourth century B.C., and it means "flower of Zeus."

The ancient Romans loved carnations for their spicy fragrance as well as for their

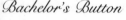
Bachelor's Button

Carnation

Chrysanthemum

beauty. One story tells that the armies of Julius Caesar spread carnations through Europe as far as Britain—by accidentally carrying the seeds in the mud on their boots. It's more likely, however, that carnations spread at a later date and by more usual means.

However they arrived in Britain, carnations became favorites with British gardeners in the Middle Ages. They were called by another name—gillyflower, which means clove flower—because the scent and flavor of carnations mimicked that of cloves, at that time a rare and valued spice. Carnations were often used as flavoring in beer, ale, and wine.

The origin of the name "carnation" is unclear. The name may come from the Latin word *carne* ("flesh"), for the pink color of early carnations. Then again, the English poet Edmund Spenser called the flower "coronation," and some people think that may have been the origin of the name.

CHRYSANTHEMUM

The name "chrysanthemum" comes from two Greek words meaning "golden flower." Some chrysanthemums are golden-colored, but among the 150 different types of this flower there are many colors and sizes. One characteristic they share, however, is that each flower has many, many petals.

Chrysanthemums have long been honored in Asia, where they are said to symbolize long life, purity, and perfection. In Japan, the Order of the Chrysanthemum is the highest honor that can be awarded to a person. And a Chinese legend tells how the first chrysanthemum came to be.

According to the tale, a young girl named Golden Flower was soon to be married to her sweetheart. But she was plagued by one worry: How long would her marriage last? One day she spotted an elf sleeping under a bush. Knowing that an elf must answer truthfully the first question put to him by a mortal, she woke him up and asked how many years she would be married.

"As many years as the flower you choose has petals," replied the elf, who was annoyed that he had been caught napping. Then he vanished.

The girl set out to find a flower with as many petals as possible. But try as she might, the best she could find was a flower with seventeen petals—not nearly enough, to her mind. Finally, she had an idea. She took the flower and, plucking a hairpin from her hair, slit each petal again and again, until the flower had dozens and dozens of petals.

Golden Flower and her sweetheart were married and lived a long and happy life together. They planted the flower, and all its descendants were many-petaled, too.

FORGET-ME-NOT

The tiny blue forget-me-nots that bloom by streams and ponds have a rich history. There are also many legends surrounding their name. One of the best-known stories tells of a German knight who walked along the bank of a river with his beloved. Spotting the pretty blue flowers of the plant, he climbed down the riverbank to pick them but fell into the swift-flowing stream. As the water swept him away, he managed to toss the flowers to the lady, crying out, "Forget me not!"

However the forget-me-not got its common name, its scientific name is based on the way its leaves look. The name is *Myosotis*, which comes from Greek words that mean "mouse's ear."

Forget-me-nots became an important symbol in English history in the late 1300's, when the nobleman Henry of Lancaster chose them as one of his emblems. Henry fell into disfavor with King Richard II, who exiled him in 1398 and then confiscated his estates. But a year later, Henry and his supporters invaded England and took control of the throne. As King Henry IV, Henry of Lancaster continued to use forget-me-nots as an emblem. They appeared in embroidery on his clothes and on enameled metal collars worn by his supporters.

GOLDENROD

This common roadside wildflower—often considered a weed when it takes hold in the garden—figures in many old superstitions. Some people believe that if goldenrod springs up near a house where people haven't planted it, good fortune is sure to come to the people who live there. Others say that treasure is buried where goldenrod blooms.

Some people have used the stalks of goldenrod plants as divining rods to search for precious minerals or water below the ground. A person walks slowly over the ground, holding out the stalk. When the stalk tips down, according to this belief, it's time to start digging.

Goldenrod is one of the many plants that were once used to make medicines for everything from chest pains to ulcers. On the other

Goldenrod

Forget-Me-Not

Marigold

Iris

hand, the most commonly held belief about goldenrod in times past was that it caused an illness: hay fever. It's easy to see why people believed this—every year when the goldenrod bloomed, people who suffered from allergies to pollen would start to sniffle and sneeze. But today we know that goldenrod was falsely accused. Another common plant, ragweed, blooms at the same time that goldenrod does. Its flowers are so inconspicuous that no one notices them—but its pollen is often to blame for hay fever.

IRIS

There are many varieties of this flower, from tall bearded irises to the smaller water irises, which are also called flags. Irises are among the oldest garden flowers—records show they were grown in ancient Egypt and ancient Greece, where they were used to decorate tombs. In Greek mythology, Iris was the goddess of the rainbow.

Iris flowers were also the basis of the fleur-de-lis, the symbol of French kings. Their association with the French throne is said to have begun in the 400's, when Clovis was

king of the Franks. According to legend, a hostile force invaded Frankish territory and pressed Clovis' army to the banks of the Rhine River. The king thought he was trapped—until he saw a stand of yellow flags growing in the water. That told him that the river was shallow enough to ford. He was able to escape his enemies, circle around, and defeat them.

In celebration, Clovis redesigned his banner to show three yellow flags, symbolizing faith, wisdom, and bravery. Hundreds of years later, when the French King Louis VII organized the Second Crusade, he chose the same emblem and covered his banners with stylized irises. Thus the design became known as the fleur (flower) de Louis—or, over time, fleur-de-lis.

MARIGOLD

"Marigold" is a name that's been given to many different flowers. The ones we're most familiar with today are the marsh marigold, a yellow wildflower that blooms near streams and bogs in early spring; the pot marigold, a garden flower that is also called

Narcissus

Violet

the calendula; and the French and African marigolds—both of which actually originated in Mexico.

"Calendula" comes from *kalends,* the Roman term for the first day of the month. The flowers of the calendula were supposed to open on that day every month of the year. The English named the calendula "pot marigold" because they once used its petals as seasoning in soups and stews. The petals were even dried and stored in barrels for use in winter. Early colonists took seeds of the plant to North America, and it was blooming in colonial gardens by the mid-1600's.

The flowers we call French and African marigolds were already firmly established in the New World by then. Spanish explorers found the French marigold growing wild in Mexico, while the African marigold was cultivated by the Aztecs. It's thought that the Aztecs honored their dead with gifts of marigolds, because this flower has been called *flor del muerto* in Mexico.

The Spanish took both types back to Spain. The plants quickly spread—the wild type to France, and the cultivated type to

North Africa. Later, other Europeans "discovered" these flowers growing in their new habitats and named them for those places.

NARCISSUS

Narcissus are delicately scented flowers that bloom in the spring. The blossoms are white or yellow, with six petals surrounding a trumpet-shaped tube. Daffodils and jonquils are considered kinds of narcissus.

The narcissus is another ancient flower—it was used in funeral wreaths in ancient Egypt more than 3,500 years ago. The Romans believed that its sweet fragrance could put people to sleep, and it has long been used in perfume.

There are also many myths about the origin of this flower. The best known is the Greek tale of the boy named Narcissus. One day, while he was out hunting in the forest, Narcissus leaned over a pool to take a drink and was captivated by the reflection of his own handsome face—in fact, he fell in love with his image and couldn't bear to stop looking at it. He died right there at the side of the pool, and the gods turned him into a narcissus flower. Today people who are too concerned with themselves are sometimes said to be narcissistic.

TULIP

This popular garden flower is wrapped in Turkish history. By the mid-1500's, Turkish sultans had conquered North Africa, the Middle East, and large parts of eastern and southern Europe. Ferdinand I, the ruler of Austria, sent an ambassador to the Turkish court in 1554 to arrange peace terms. The ambassador succeeded in winning peace— and he was also delighted by the Turkish gardens that he saw. Growing there were brilliant red and yellow flowers that looked like the turbans, or *tulibands,* worn by Turkish men. The ambassador called the flowers *tulipans* and took some back to Vienna, to be planted in the royal gardens.

Tulips spread and, over time, became the rage in European gardens, especially the gardens of Holland. At first the bulbs were cheap, so everyone could afford to plant them. Then, in the 1600's, a strange thing happened. Some of the bulbs began to produce flowers with streaks and combinations of colors. Because these bulbs were so rare, people were willing to pay huge amounts of money for them.

The changes in the flowers were caused by a virus spread by insects. But growers tried all sorts of formulas to make tulip bulbs change and produce new types of flowers, including soaking the seeds in ink. For a few years, ''tulipomania'' gripped Holland, and fortunes were made and lost by speculating in tulip bulbs. Today, the tulip's many different sizes, shapes, and color combinations are achieved mostly through hybridization.

VIOLET

Violets are woodland plants that have become favorites in shady gardens. The way the small purple flowers peek out from under the broad leaves has led people to use words like ''shy'' and ''modest'' to describe them.

According to legend, violets were created by the Greek god Zeus. It's told that Zeus fell in love with a woman named Io—and his wife, Hera, became enraged. He was forced to change Io into a pure white heifer to protect her from Hera's wrath. Saddened by his act, he decided to give Io a special diet. He waved his hand, and violets sprang up.

The Greeks believed that a wreath of violets, worn around the head, would bring pleasant dreams. Later, in Germany, violets were thought to bring good luck and were used to decorate cradles. In France during the time of Napoleon, violets also became an important symbol. Napoleon was sometimes called Corporal Violette, and his supporters wore violets to show their loyalty.

Thus the shy violet, like so many other flowers, has fascinating tales to tell.

Tulip

A BIRTHDAY PARTY FOR SNOW WHITE

In 1937, the Walt Disney studio released a film that was unlike any that had ever been shown before. The film was *Snow White and the Seven Dwarfs,* and it was the very first feature-length animated cartoon.

At the time, people thought Disney was mad—audiences would never sit through a feature-length cartoon, they predicted. But audiences quickly proved the doubters wrong: *Snow White* became one of the most popular films of all time. In 1987, the Disney studio celebrated *Snow White*'s 50th anniversary with a host of special events, and audiences flocked to see it once again. In the years since its making, the film has come to be regarded as a true classic.

A DARING VENTURE

Snow White is based on a Grimm brothers fairy tale that tells of a princess, Snow White, whose wicked stepmother orders her killed. She takes refuge in the forest with a group of dwarfs, but her stepmother finds her and poisons her. Then a handsome prince appears and kisses her. She awakens, and they live happily ever after.

When Walt Disney decided to make a film based on this tale in 1934, he was met with a chorus of objections. Not only was the idea of a feature-length animated film outlandish, but fantasies were notorious box-office flops. Adults wouldn't want to see a fairy tale, and

children—well, their ticket purchases would never cover the estimated $250,000 it would cost to make the film.

Nonetheless, Disney went ahead.

Critical in the early stages was the process of developing the characters. Dozens of Snow Whites were drawn and rejected, and the final design was refined again and again. In the end, the character of Snow White was a breakthrough—the first cartoon figure to seem human. The dwarfs also received careful attention, right down to their names. (The dwarfs in the original fairy tale have no names.) The Disney team considered and rejected dwarf characters with names such as Hotsy and Shifty before settling on the now-famous seven—Sneezy, Sleepy, Dopey, Happy, Bashful, Grumpy, and Doc.

Each character also needed a voice, and dozens of actors were auditioned for these parts. Snow White's voice was provided by Adriana Caselotti. But when the studio couldn't find an appropriate voice for Dopey, it decided to let him remain silent throughout the film.

In all, nine story adapters, two character developers, six directors, seven background painters, ten art directors, and twenty-eight animators worked on the film. (Disney himself did none of the drawing.) Animators took months to produce each scene of the movie, studying films of live actors and pains-

Snow White and the Seven Dwarfs was the first feature-length animated cartoon and one of the most popular films of all time. It celebrated its 50th anniversary in 1987.

takingly drawing each frame for the most lifelike effect. The animated figures were then combined with painted backgrounds.

Music was also an important part of the film, and several composers worked on it. *Snow White* included several songs that became famous—the dwarfs' march, with its "heigh-ho" refrain, Snow White's "Some Day My Prince Will Come" and "Whistle While You Work." But Disney also used background music to help move the story along. Each character had a separate musical theme—romantic themes for Snow White and her prince; an evil, brooding theme for the wicked Queen; and comic themes for the dwarfs.

The final cost of the picture was far more than had been estimated—$1.5 million. Most of the money was borrowed, putting the studio on shaky ground. But if Disney worried about turning a profit on the film, he needn't have. It opened in Hollywood on December 21, 1937, and was an instant hit. *Snow White* earned more than $8 million in its first year, becoming the biggest box-office money-maker of its time.

A CLASSIC IS BORN

Snow White also earned rave reviews from critics. The famous comic Charlie Chaplin called Dopey "one of the greatest comedians of all time." A New York critic wrote, "It is a classic. . . . If you miss it, you'll be missing the 10 best pictures of 1938." Soon *Snow White* was drawing audiences in some 40 countries, with soundtracks in ten languages. The film was *Blanche-Neige et les Sept Nains* in France, and *Schneewittchen und die Sieben Dwerge* in Germany.

In fact, the film never lost its popularity. Disney (and other filmmakers) made many other full-length cartoon features. But whenever *Snow White* was shown again, audiences turned out in huge numbers. By the time the film turned 50, it had earned some $330 million worldwide.

The Disney studio celebrated *Snow White*'s anniversary by declaring 1987 the "Year of Snow White." There were "Snow White" parades at the Disney theme parks —Disneyland in California and Walt Disney World in Florida. Entertainers dressed as Snow White and the dwarfs toured children's hospitals and made special appearances at the New York Stock Exchange, the Smithsonian Institution, and even at the White House Easter Egg Roll. *Snow White* commemorative coins and a special *Snow White* rose were produced. And a brass star bearing Snow White's name was embedded in a Hollywood sidewalk, next to stars with the names of live actors.

Meanwhile, the film itself was released again in 60 countries. Audiences around the world found that on screen, Snow White hardly looked her age—she seemed as fresh and charming as ever. Her prince was just as handsome, the evil Queen just as threatening, and the dwarfs just as lovable as they had been 50 years before.

As part of the birthday celebrations, entertainers dressed as Snow White and the dwarfs made appearances at children's hospitals, the Smithsonian Institution, and the New York Stock Exchange (*shown here*).

PARROTS: PERSONALITY PLUS

Parrots are the clowns of the bird world, a three-ring circus all in themselves. In the wild, they fly through the air in noisy flocks and clamber about like acrobats in the trees. In captivity, they are prized for their beauty and cleverness—including, sometimes, the ability to mimic human speech.

The parrots that are most familiar are the brightly colored birds often seen in pet stores. They range from common parakeets to exotic macaws and cockatoos. But these birds are just a few of the hundreds of different kinds of parrots that live in the wild. Many are rare, and some are in danger of dying out. Their popularity with people has increased their problems, since they are often captured and sold as pets.

PARROTS IN THE WILD

Parrots are found in warm regions all over the world, but they are most common in Central and South America, South Asia, the South Pacific, and Australia and New Zea-land. Europe is the only continent with no native parrots, although fossil records show that parrots once lived there. One American type, the Carolina parakeet, once ranged as far north as Virginia and Ohio. But this bird is now extinct.

Parrots vary greatly in size—some are smaller than sparrows and some are as much as 3 feet (1 meter) long. Many are strikingly colored, although a few are dull green or even black. But all parrots share certain traits, the most distinctive of which is a powerful, sharply hooked beak. Some parrots can easily crack nuts with their beaks. And

This page: left—masked lovebirds; right—scarlet macaw. Opposite page: top left—African gray parrot; top right—rainbow lorikeets; bottom—pink cockatoo.

nearly all use their beaks as an aid in climbing, pulling themselves up tree trunks with this "third foot."

Parrots also have unusual feet. Most birds have three toes pointing forward and one toe pointing back, but parrots have two toes pointing in each direction. Their feet act like pincers, which also helps them climb. And unlike other birds, some parrots can use their feet like hands to hold food. But the odd toe configuration makes them wobble comically when they walk on the ground.

Some people believe that parrots are among the most intelligent birds. They are also highly sociable, gathering in pairs and flocks to roost and feed each day. They're noisy when they gather—their raucous calls fill the air and can be heard miles away.

While the flock is feeding, one parrot will often serve as a lookout, alerting the others with a scream if a predator approaches. Most parrots are vegetarians, eating fruits, nuts, seeds, flowers, grasses, and other plants. Many also eat insects. Parrots have fleshy tongues and appear to have a good sense of taste; they often test food before eating it.

Most parrots prefer to build their nests in cavities, such as a hole in a tree trunk. A few use burrows in the ground, and some Austra-

in two ways: It's nocturnal (active at night), and it can't fly. Owl parrots are native to New Zealand. As the name suggests, their bristlelike feathers around the beak make them look more like owls than parrots.

• Another rare species, the **vulturine parrot**, takes after a different bird. With a ruff of feathers around its neck, this crow-sized parrot looks like a vulture.

• Like the owl parrot, the **kea** and its close relative the **kaka** live in New Zealand. These are large, aggressive birds with sharp beaks. The kea is unusual among parrots because it occasionally attacks sheep. But its usual diet is composed of insects and roots.

• The **lories** and **lorikeets** of Australia and the South Pacific include nearly 60 different species. They are small birds with brilliantly colored plumage, and they are among the most beautiful of all the parrots. They have relatively slender bills and use their tongues, which are rough and furry, to feed on the nectar of flowers.

• **Hanging parrots** are small birds with an unusual habit: They sleep hanging head down, like bats, from the branches of trees. (Although sleeping upside down is rare, some other parrot species like to hang head down to bathe.) Hanging parrots are native to Southeast Asia, and there are some ten species.

• The **pygmy parrots** of New Guinea live up to their name—some are no bigger than a man's thumb. The half dozen species have short, stiff tails that they use to brace themselves as they inch up and down tree trunks.

• **Cockatoos** are big birds, with large heads topped by crests of feathers. These birds can expand their crests like fans, for a spectacular display. There are sixteen different species, some white with pink or yellow crests and a few completely black. Found in Australia, New Guinea, and elsewhere in South Asia, cockatoos sometimes gather in flocks of thousands and can cause considerable damage to crops.

• **True parrots** are the largest group, with some two hundred different species found around the world. The most familiar are probably the **Amazon parrots**, square-tailed green birds that are often marked with yellow, red, or blue. True parrots also include the flashy **macaws**, long-tailed birds in hues that range from scarlet to brilliant greens,

lian types dig nesting holes in termite mounds. Many kinds of parrots mate for life. They may breed once or twice a year, and both parents help care for the newly hatched chicks.

KINDS OF PARROTS

There are more than 300 different species (types) of parrots, and all belong to the family *Psittacidae*. Scientists have divided them into eight groups, or subfamilies:

• The **owl parrot** is in a group by itself. This bird is extremely rare—in fact, it's close to extinction. The owl parrot is unique

yellows, and blues. Macaws, which are found in Central and South America, are the largest parrots. And the great blue hyacinth macaw of Brazil is the largest macaw.

Parakeets are also part of the true parrot group. The most familiar parakeets belong to two Australian groups, the ground parakeets and the grass parakeets. Ground parakeets never roost in trees; they even build their nests on the ground. One of the grass parakeets, the **budgerigar**, is the familiar parakeet seen in pet stores.

Lovebirds, native to Africa, are still another kind of true parrot. These small birds earned their name from their habit of mating for life and spending much of their time cuddling up to each other. But it's likely that the birds are just preening each other, not showing true affection.

PARROTS AND PEOPLE

People have been fascinated by parrots for thousands of years, and these birds were among the earliest domesticated animals. They were brought from Asia to Europe in the time of Alexander the Great. The ancient Romans kept parrots as pets, although parrots also showed up as entrées at Roman banquets. Tame parrots were kept by Indians in South and Central America, too.

The birds' cleverness and bright colors account for some of their popularity with people. But what fascinates people most about parrots is probably their ability to mimic human speech. The African gray parrot is famous for its ability to "talk." Many other types, including Amazon parrots and even parakeets, have also been taught to repeat words and phrases. But it's highly unlikely that parrots have any understanding of what they say—to them, the words are just sounds. Teaching a parrot to speak requires great patience because the words must be repeated over and over again.

Parakeets and lovebirds make fine pets, but larger parrots can be difficult ones. While many are docile, they can be noisy, unpredictable, and sometimes destructive. They can't be kept in small cages—they need room to stretch their wings. Like many other birds, parrots also carry psittacosis, a disease that can be transmitted to humans, and other diseases that can spread to poultry. For that reason, every bird imported to the

United States and Canada must be inspected and held in quarantine.

Despite these difficulties, large parrots remain popular as pets. And that popularity has created other problems. Many species are becoming rare in their natural habitats. This is partly because many are captured and sold as pets, but even more because the tropical forests where they live are being destroyed as civilization advances.

Some types of parrots are bred for sale as pets. But other types are rare, and they sell for thousands of dollars in pet stores. A hyacinth macaw or a palm cockatoo, for example, can cost as much as $6,000. It may not be possible to obtain a rare parrot at all, since many countries limit or forbid the capture and export of these birds.

Still, the demand for parrots is so great that some people smuggle captured birds. The smuggled birds are often mistreated, and many die. Others may be carrying disease. For these reasons, wildlife experts say that people shouldn't buy rare parrots or keep them as pets. These clever, colorful birds should be allowed to live free in the wild.

Parrots can easily crack nuts with their powerful hooked beaks. And some use their feet like hands to hold food.

FANCIFUL FLOATERS

A flying elephant? Uncle Sam in the sky? Of course. Anything's possible in the adventurous world of ballooning. Always colorful, hot-air balloons now have a new feature: Many are unique and fanciful creations.

Some unusual balloons are designed for special events. The flying elephant, for example, was made for a goodwill tour of Asian countries (it's shown here over Brunei, a country on the island of Borneo).

Other eye-catching balloons are used as advertising messages. You may recognize Tony the Tiger at right—he's associated with a breakfast cereal. And still other balloons are made simply to stand out in a crowd—such as the face below. Called Miss Chic I. Boom, the balloon is modeled on Carmen Miranda, a well-known singer of the 1940's who wore hats adorned with fake fruit.

Next time you spot a hot-air balloon floating in the sky, take a closer look. It may be someone—or something—you know.

TV TURN-ON

It's a scene played out in homes everywhere, day after day: You come home from school and flick on the television. Then your mother or father walks in and says, "Why are you wasting your time with that junk?"

The quality of television programs, especially programs for children, is something that's constantly debated. In recent years, however, a few children's programs have broken out of the standard mold. Some, taking their cue from public television's long-popular "Sesame Street," seek to combine entertainment with education. They include "Square One TV," "3-2-1 Contact," and "Owl/TV." Another show, "Faerie Tale Theatre," brings top actors, directors, and writers to productions that are designed especially for kids.

MAKING MATH FUN

"Square One TV" made its debut on public television in 1987. It was developed for 8- to 12-year-olds by Children's Television Workshop, the group that created "Sesame Street" to entertain younger children while teaching the basics of reading. And what "Sesame Street" does for reading, "Square One" tries to do for math.

The idea of the show is to use bright, jazzy entertainment to conquer "math phobia"—the dread of the subject that makes many students avoid it. Unlike classroom instruction, the show doesn't concentrate on teaching children specific mathematical methods. Instead, it tries to show that math can be both useful and fun.

"Square One" does this through fast-paced skits and songs. Take the subject of combinatorics—an intimidating name for the mathematical principles that govern the ways in which different objects or numbers can be combined. The show makes this subject fun and understandable with a skit in which the **Battle of the Bulge Caterers** figure the possibilities of combining ham, turkey, and American, Swiss, and provolone cheese in sandwiches.

Mathman, an animated segment that echoes the video game Pac-Man, uses dot-gobbling characters to introduce the properties of numbers, such as which numbers are multiples of three. Ancient Romans show up at a pop-music recording session to introduce Roman numerals. And problems in mathematical logic are presented in riddles.

Many of the skits are send-ups of other television shows. A segment called **Mathnet** is a takeoff on the old detective series "Dragnet." In this version, however, the deadpan detectives solve problems through

"Square One TV" teaches basic math concepts through jazzy skits that often parody other TV shows.

Using a magazine format and weekly themes, "3-2-1 Contact" makes the world of science and technology come alive.

mathematical logic. And a takeoff on "American Bandstand" features characters straight out of "Star Trek" and teaches the basics of averaging.

In the 75 "Square One" shows shown in 1987, seven regular actors played dozens of roles, and guests also appeared. The daily shows were so lively that some critics faulted them for being too entertaining—and not concentrating enough on education. But the show's producers say that entertainment must come first—if no one watches the show, it won't help anyone learn.

FOCUS ON SCIENCE

When "Square One" made its debut, another Children's Television Workshop show was in its fifth season. This was "3-2-1 Contact," a show that aims to make science and technology exciting and understandable to 8- to 12-year-olds.

The show uses a "magazine" format, in which young hosts travel around the world in search of scientific information. Film shot on location and in the studio, documentaries, animation, and music make up each daily episode. Each week's episodes share a common theme, such as space, electricity, light, farms, or flight.

For the 1986–87 season, there were four new themes: signals, oceans, motion, and eating. During **signals week**, American Indians demonstrated hand signals, and shepherds from the Pyrenees Mountains in France showed how they communicate over long distances by whistling. The shows also featured some modern signals: picture-phones in use in Biarritz, France, and computer signals that help put out a newspaper.

Oceans week explored such questions as why the oceans are salty, what an oceanographer does, and how to move a whale from one tank to another (by crane). Segments showed the young cast members exploring a sunken Civil War paddle wheeler off the coast of Bermuda and swimming with penguins at Sea World in San Diego, California.

Motion week examined the forces of nature that influence motion—for example, how a snake uses friction to move, and how reducing friction enables a French train to travel at more than 200 miles (320 kilometers) an hour. One cast member demonstrated how levers and pulleys work by using them to lift another cast member. And a veterinarian explained how anatomy affects the ways animals move. Elephants, for example, don't jump—because they're just not built to.

During **eating week**, the show focused on how people and animals obtain, process, and

"Owl/TV" is a fast-paced nature and science series that is based on the popular Canadian children's magazine.

use food. Films showed how special zoo diets are prepared and then gave a close-up look at some picky eaters: koalas, zebras, pygmy hippos, and lesser pandas. The show also had archeologists analyzing the diet of people who lived 6,000 years ago in Texas. What did they eat? Lizards, insects, rodents, and flowers!

"3-2-1 Contact" had some other new features for its fifth season. One was a series of short comments by famous scientists, who talked about what had sparked their interest in science when they were youngsters. And for the first time, the show produced some segments jointly with a French television network, for broadcast in both countries. In all, "3-2-1 Contact" has been broadcast in 32 countries.

DISCOVERING NATURE

"Owl/TV," a nature and science discovery series for 7- to 12-year-olds, is the television version of the popular Canadian children's nature magazine *Owl*. The weekly series entered its second season in 1986–87. Produced in Canada, it is also aired by U.S. public broadcasting stations.

Each half-hour show is divided into four segments, linked by fast-paced mini-features and jokes. The segments show young people exploring the world of animals, the environment, and science. They're chosen from seven recurring features that are based on feature departments in the magazine.

The Mighty Mites are three children who shrink (with the help of trick photography) to explore microscopic environments. In some episodes, they've been seen inching their way up leaves and swimming in a fish tank with guppies.

Fooling Around With Science features Dr. Zed, a brilliant (if eccentric-looking) scientist. He guides young visitors through a range of experiments, from turning milk into cheese to splitting light into the colors of the rainbow.

Animals Close Up explores the animal world. Kids go on location to interview zoologists and other experts on animals, and they meet the animals firsthand. One show visited an unusual laboratory in New Mexico —a laboratory where bats are studied.

Tomorrow/Today looks into the future. The show travels to working laboratories where the technologies and products that will influence the future are being developed. One of these features showed how cars of the future are being designed, and another explored the medical uses of snake venom.

You and Your Body features one of the show's most popular stars: Bonapart, a joke-cracking skeleton whose eyes light up when he speaks. He helps viewers unravel such mysteries as the workings of the inner ear and the skin.

Real Kids focuses on young people who are working to improve the environment. The cases featured on the show are real, and they help demonstrate that individuals of any age can improve their world.

The Hoot Club is the final segment of each show. Here, club members work together on a project—anything from making scarecrows to building an inflatable spaceship.

In some of the 1986–87 shows, viewers saw what it was like to travel by dogsled in the Arctic, track hibernating bears, visit Pueblo Indians in New Mexico, and watch a llama being born.

HAPPILY EVER AFTER

"Faerie Tale Theatre" has been broadcast on the cable television network Showtime since 1982. Each show in the series is an hour-long production of a famous fairy tale.

Among the more than two dozen that have been presented are "The Princess and the Pea," "Rumplestiltskin," "Hansel and Gretel," "Sleeping Beauty," "Pinocchio," "Cinderella," and "The Snow Queen."

What makes these presentations truly special is their high level of acting, directing, and production. The show was the brainchild of the actress and producer Shelley Duvall, who called on her contacts to help carry out the idea. Among the well-known performers who have appeared in the series are Joan Collins, Robin Williams, Liza Minnelli, Christopher Reeve, James Earl Jones, and Vanessa Redgrave. Directors have included Francis Ford Coppola and Roger Vadim.

The show enlists top writers in the film industry to rewrite the tales for television, and top designers to develop sets based on the works of such famous artists and illustrators as Maxfield Parrish and N. C. Wyeth. Special video effects add to the settings, creating an underwater world for "The Little Mermaid," for example, and lending a dreamlike quality to "Rip Van Winkle."

All the effort put into the productions has helped make "Faerie Tale Theatre" one of the most praised children's shows on television. The many awards the show has won leave no doubt: Children's television can be good—and good for you, too.

"The Little Mermaid" and other high-quality presentations have made "Faerie Tale Theatre" a hit with kids.

COOKIE CUTTER CARDS

The next time you need a greeting card, make your own. It's a personal and fun way to tell people that you think they're extra special.

One way to make greeting cards is by using cookie cutters. Cutters are available in many different designs, which can be used singly or in groups.

Make the card itself from colorful construction paper. First, fold the paper in half so that it opens like a greeting card. Then position the cookie cutter on the underside of the card's front page and trace around the cutter. Cut along the lines, leaving a hole in

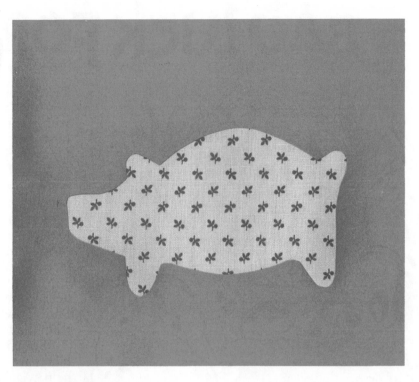

the card. Back this hole with construction paper of another color—or with patterned wrapping paper or fabric.

To give the inside of the card a neat appearance, cut out a piece of construction paper that's almost as large as the front of the card. Glue this over the complete underside, thus covering the material used for the design.

You may want to draw borders and other decorations on the front of the card. Use a felt-tip marker to give a dinosaur an eye, or bits of construction paper to jazz up a gingerbread man.

Now write your message on the inside of the card—"Happy Birthday," "Thanks!" or just simply "Hi, friend."

BAD LUCK FOR LUCKY

"Aw, that was just a movie," said Lucky with a shrug. He stashed the object under a bush and joined his brothers in the kitchen for a snack.

When Lucky bounded through the door, Nanny greeted him with a frown. "You naughty pup," she scolded, wagging her finger at him. "You've been digging again. Just look at your dirty paws."

So while everyone else ate biscuits and lapped milk, Lucky got a bath and a lecture.

Nanny was still toweling him dry when he heard the sounds of "The Thunderbolt Show," which was drifting into the kitchen from the living-room television set.

"Stop fidgeting," ordered Nanny, rubbing him hard with the towel. Lucky couldn't help wiggling as he heard his brothers and sisters cheering for Thunderbolt the Wonder Dog.

Dirt flew in all directions as Lucky plunged deeper into the hole he was digging.

"It's time for our snack," chorused two puppy voices.

Lucky's head popped up to see his brothers, Rolly and Patch, watching him.

"I've almost got it," he cried, and dived back into the hole. When he came up again, something dangled from his mouth. He gave it a few quick shakes and dropped it at Patch's feet.

"There!" he said proudly. "What do you think of it?"

"What is it?" asked Patch as he sniffed at it.

"I don't know, but I think it's gold. And it's real old."

Rolly looked at it closely. "It's got writing on it," he noticed. "Maybe it's an ancient relic and the writing is an evil spell—like in that movie we saw on television, *The Egyptian Ring*. Remember? The king who owned the ring had horrible things happen to him!"

A few final rubs and Nanny put Lucky down on the kitchen floor. He took off like a shot, not wanting to miss one more minute of his favorite show. Down the hall he went, and skidded around the corner into the living room. His paws dug at the carpet, but Lucky couldn't stop his skid. He hit a table leg with a dull thud. Then came a loud crash.

When Nanny rounded the corner, she found Lucky sitting among the broken remains of a flower vase.

"Lucky!" she cried. "You know you mustn't run in the house!" And Nanny carried him back to the kitchen and plopped him down in a corner.

Lucky moped in the kitchen while his brothers and sisters watched the television show. When it was over, Patch and Rolly joined him.

"I told you that thing you found had an evil spell on it," said Rolly. "Look at all the trouble you've been in today."

"What are you going to do?" asked Patch.

Lucky had had the whole "Thunderbolt" show to think about it. "I'm going to bury it again—somewhere else," he said firmly. "Then maybe the bad luck will leave me."

"We can bury it in the park tonight," suggested Rolly. "That should be far enough away."

That night, when everyone was asleep, the three pups slipped quietly out the back door. The moon was just a sliver in the sky, and a gentle breeze rustled the trees as they took turns digging a hole under the fence in the yard.

Lucky was the first to squeeze through, holding the relic gingerly between his teeth. Patch followed, calling back to Rolly, "Hurry! It's getting late."

He was answered by a yelp. "I can't get through," cried Rolly. His head was on one side of the fence, but his chubby body was on the other.

"We haven't got time to dig a deeper hole," said Patch, turning toward the park. "You'll have to stay here."

Rolly inched back into the yard and sat down. He peered through the iron fence as Patch and Lucky disappeared down the street.

By the time Lucky and Patch reached the park, the tiny moon had disappeared behind a passing cloud, and the trees lining the path loomed dark against a darker sky.

"The park sure looks different at night," said Patch with a shudder. They both quickened their steps.

It didn't take Lucky long to find a clear space near the path. Patch stood guard while Lucky scratched a shallow hole and dropped the relic into it. He was about to cover it over when Patch growled in a low voice, "I hear footsteps."

Lucky sat up, ears forward, listening. "I hear them, too," he whispered. "And they're not coming down the path. They're coming through the bushes."

Both pups peered at the bushes, but all they could see was a black tangle of branches that formed strange shapes. The footsteps came closer.

"I'm afraid," whispered Patch in a trembling voice.

Lucky was, too, but he summoned his courage and barked, "Who's there?"

No one answered. Then the footsteps began moving faster. Lucky could hear the branches snap as whatever it was moved toward them. It sounded large and horrible.

"It's the Egyptian spell!" groaned Patch, who was backing down the path. The bushes began to shake, moving back and forth, and a small white shadow leaped out onto the path.

"Boy, am I glad to see you guys!" panted Rolly. "I finally got through the fence, but then I got lost in the park. If you hadn't barked, Lucky, I would never have found you and Patch."

Then Rolly noticed how quiet his brothers were. "What's the matter?" he asked. "You look like you've seen a ghost."

"Never mind," said Lucky. "Let's get out of here." And they all ran for home.

The next afternoon, when "Thunderbolt" was over, Roger and Anita took Pongo, Perdita, and the puppies for a walk in the park —all except Lucky, Patch, and Rolly, who were curled up sleeping soundly in front of the silent television set.

Lucky was dreaming about ancient relics and angry Egyptian priests when he awoke with a start. Roger had burst through the door, followed by the rest of the family.

"Nanny!" he called out. "Look what Pongo found in the park."

Lucky was horrified to see Roger holding up the relic he had buried in the park. Now Pongo would have bad luck!

"What on earth is that?" Nanny asked, taking the object from Roger and turning it over carefully in her hand.

"It's a medal of valor that belonged to my father," said Roger in an excited voice. "The one I thought Pongo had buried in the backyard when he was a pup."

Roger reached down and gave Pongo a pat on the head. "I still can't imagine what it was doing in the park," he said, scratching his head. "Oh, well. I have it back again. This must be my lucky day."

"Mine, too," thought Lucky. And he breathed a sigh of relief.

WETLAND WILDERNESSES

Tall marsh grasses bend in a soft breeze, revealing patches of glimmering water at their roots. An egret wades delicately through the grass, while a flock of ducks soars overhead. Nearby a muskrat paddles down a channel, only its head visible above the water. The air is filled with the song of birds and the hum of countless insects.

This peaceful scene is taking place in a wetland. A wetland is an area where the soil is saturated with water, and water is the main factor in determining the kinds of soil and plant and animal life that are found there. There are wetlands all over the world. They form inland, in shallow lakes and ponds that fill with silt and in areas where the land is depressed into bowls that trap water; and along the seacoast, when the ocean water recedes.

People have long considered wetlands to be waste areas because they are unsuitable for building or farming. For that reason, people have often drained them, filled them in, and destroyed them. Now, however, people have begun to appreciate the true value of these rich and varied areas, and they are working to protect them.

Wetlands of various kinds provide homes for a rich variety of plant and animal life. They are also important to surrounding areas. In heavy rains they help control floods by holding back water. In times of drought, they act as water reserves. Some wetlands act as water filters, trapping pollutants from rivers and streams and allowing them to be cleaned out.

Wetlands include marshes like the one described above, as well as bogs and swamps. The lines between these types of wetlands aren't clearly drawn, and many people use the terms interchangeably. But there are distinct differences between the types.

MARSHES

Marshes are generally described as open, watery areas with tall grasslike plants. There are two basic types: inland, freshwater marshes, which form when shallow lakes and ponds begin to fill in with silt; and tidal, or saltwater, marshes, which form along coastal areas.

The specific plants and animals living in marshes vary depending on where the marsh is located. In North America, cattails, sedges, waterlilies, and various pondweeds grow in the freshwater marshes. Freshwater marshes are also home to intriguing insect-eating plants. These include pitcher plants, which drown insects in tube-shaped leaves half-filled with water; sundews, which catch insects on leaves covered with sticky projections; and bladderworts, water plants that capture underwater insects in tiny, balloon-shaped ''bladders,'' or sacs. The plants have no lack of prey—dragonflies, midges, mosquitoes, and many other insects abound in the marsh.

Freshwater marshes are also rich in other animal life. Clams, crayfish, and many kinds of fish live in the water. Frogs, salamanders, turtles, lizards, and snakes hop, crawl, and slither through the grass. Ducks and geese make their homes in the marsh and often raise their young there. So do blackbirds, wading birds such as herons and egrets, and predators such as hawks and owls. Muskrats, beavers, raccoons, rabbits, rats, foxes, mink, deer—and even, in some areas, bears—visit or live in marshes.

In the tidal marshes, the plants are limited to those that can tolerate the brackish, salty water. They include cord grass and various kinds of rushes. Besides the usual marsh birds and animals, there are oysters, crabs, shrimp, snails, and gulls and other seabirds. Tidal marshes are hatcheries for many kinds of fish—experts say that 80 to 90 percent of the fish sold worldwide depend on these shallow coastal waters at some point in their lives. And in North America, tidal marshes along both coasts and freshwater marshes in the center of the continent provide feeding grounds for millions of migrating birds each year.

Some marshlands are seasonal—they form in rainy seasons and dry up at other times of the year. The prairie potholes of North Dakota are an example. These ponds and marshes developed in depressions made by glaciers thousands of years ago. Some hold water all year, but others are so small that they dry up in summer. The following

A marsh is an open, watery area with tall grasslike plants. Bitterns, raccoons, and sundews (insect-eating plants with sticky leaves) are just some of the many living things that enjoy this type of wetland.

spring, however, they fill with rain and melted snow and come back to life. Snails, insect larvae, and freshwater shrimp hatch in the pools, and millions of ducks, geese, and other birds arrive to nest. By some estimates, the pothole region produces half to two thirds of the ducks in North America. But because the potholes are located in rich farming country, they are rapidly being filled in and converted to farmland.

BOGS

Bogs are generally found in northern regions, where glaciers once carved out depressions in the land. Water collects in these areas, and plants take root. But these areas are usually poorly drained and thus receive little oxygen. As the plants die, the poor drainage and lack of oxygen slow the decaying process. Some of the partly decayed plant matter floats to the surface of the water, and a mat of moss and plant stems begins to grow on top of it. The moss usually associated with bogs is sphagnum moss, which is very spongy. This floating mat of living and dead vegetation gets thicker and thicker. The mat may eventually become thick enough to support a person, but it will "quake" as the person walks.

As the water becomes choked with vegetation, some of the decaying plant material begins to accumulate on the bottom in the form of peat. The layers of peat at the bottom and the cushiony mat of plant matter on the surface are the features that separate bogs from marshes and swamps.

Both the sphagnum moss and the peat make the bog highly acidic, and this limits the kinds of plant that can live there. But plants that like an acid environment—including cranberry, sedges, heaths, reeds, the insect-eating plants, and many wildflowers—grow well in bogs. Like marshes, bogs are generally open wetlands. But some have shrubs and trees, including black spruce and white pine. Bogs also have fewer animals than marshes, although insects are just as plentiful. Warblers and other birds live in bogs, along with frogs and small mammals such as mice, voles, and lemmings.

Peat bogs hold fascinating secrets. Because of the acidity, little that falls into them decays. Human and animal remains dating back 5,000 years or more, as well as many ancient artifacts, have been found in bogs and have given researchers many clues to the past. But peat bogs serve another purpose as well. Cut into bricks and dried, peat is an excellent fuel. It has long been used in Ireland and other areas that have extensive peat bogs, and today it is even used to run some electrical power plants.

SWAMPS

Swamps differ from other wetlands chiefly because of the trees and shrubs that grow in them. They represent a later stage in the development of wetlands: The ground has filled in and dried out enough to support some species of trees. But the ground is still poorly drained and wet, with channels of dark, slow-moving water. Some trees, such as the bald cypress, grow right out of the water. Others prefer higher ground and grow on islands, or hummocks, that have been pushed up out of the swamp.

Shaded by moss-covered trees, a swamp can be a dark, spooky place. In fact, one of the largest swamps in the United States, located in North Carolina and Virginia, is called the Dismal Swamp. But swamps teem with life. Many of the same plants and animals that live in bogs and marshes also live in swamps. The huge Okefenokee Swamp, in Georgia and Florida, supports more than 200 different kinds of birds, along with 32 species of amphibians and 48 kinds of reptiles. Many of these species are rare and live only in wetland areas. Some swamps in the southern United States are home to the alligator.

There are three main kinds of swamps. In shallow-water swamps, the ground stays moist all year. Willows, alders, buttonbushes, and other trees and shrubs grow, along with ferns, vines, and many wildflowers. Shallow-water swamps may cover large tracts of land, but many are just pockets of damp ground in the middle of the forest.

Deep-water swamps form along rivers and are flooded at certain seasons. Oaks, cypresses, elms, and other tall trees—draped with hanging vines and Spanish moss—create dense shade. The bottomland hardwood forests of the lower Mississippi River Valley

A bog has a layer of peat at the bottom and a cushiony mat of plant matter, usually sphagnum moss, on the surface. A bog's acidity limits the kinds of plants and animals that live there. But frogs and many kinds of wildflowers (such as these lady's slipper orchids) find it a welcoming environment.

A swamp is a kind of wetland in which the ground has been filled in and dried out enough to support some species of trees. When the trees are covered with moss, the swamp can look dark and spooky. But swamps teem with life, and alligators and egrets are among the animals that call them home.

are typical of this kind of swamp. When they are flooded in winter, they provide breeding grounds for many waterfowl, including about a fourth of the mallard ducks in the United States.

Deep-water and shallow-water swamps are both freshwater swamps. In tropical areas, saltwater swamps sometimes develop along the seacoast. Mangrove trees grow from the water, and the swamps provide homes for pelicans and many sea creatures.

THREATENED WETLANDS

All over the world, wetlands are disappearing at an alarming rate. The United States once had some 250 million acres of wetlands. Now there are less than 100 million, and they are disappearing at a rate of more than 400,000 acres a year. Wetlands are drained for housing developments, shopping malls, and farmland; dredged to make channels for ships; and damaged by polluted water.

In the last few years, however, people have become more aware of the importance of wetlands. Besides providing flood control and water reserves, wetlands are important to the food chain because they provide breeding grounds for so many animals. And because many wetland plants and animals are rare and can live only in their water habitat, destruction of wetlands threatens many species with extinction.

In many areas, laws now protect wetlands and make it more difficult for developers and others to fill them in. Some wetland areas have been set aside as parks or nature preserves. But many of the remaining wetlands are still in danger, and so are the plants and animals that live in them.

One of the largest and richest wetlands in the United States is the Everglades, a two-million-acre expanse of swamp and other wetland areas in southern Florida. Part of the area is protected as a national park, but most is not. The story of the Everglades illustrates what can happen when people alter the delicate balance of a wetland.

The Everglades was created ages ago by drainage from Lake Okeechobee—water flows slowly in a 50-mile-wide sheet from the lake through the swamp to Florida Bay.

Until this century, the Everglades was a wetland paradise. Fish, frogs, turtles, and alligators abounded in the water. Storks, egrets, flamingos, and herons waded about, and countless waterfowl lived there. Raccoons, deer, and other animals—including the Florida panther—made their homes in the glades. Florida Bay, where fresh water from the swamp mixed with salt water from the sea, provided an ideal spawning ground for shrimp, fish, and other sea creatures.

Then, around the turn of the century, Florida began to grow. Developers began to drain the Everglades to create farmland and housing sites. They built dams and levees to control the flow of water, and canals to bring drinking water to the state's growing cities. Slowly at first, and then more quickly, the Everglades began to dry up.

By the mid-1960's, the damage was extensive. Plants and animals began to die out, and brushfires swept through areas that were once marshy. Florida Bay, no longer receiving an influx of fresh water from the swamp, became so salty that the young sea creatures that spawned there couldn't live. Salt levels began to rise in the swamp itself. And people realized that even more was at stake. Most of Florida's water supply comes from a huge underground aquifer that is constantly refilled by water that seeps down from the Everglades. With the swampland vanishing, the aquifer could dry up as well.

At first, the government tried to correct the problem by releasing vast quantities of water into the swamp at set intervals. But that only created more problems—floods alternated with dry spells, and more animals died. Now a new plan has been developed, in which water is released on a schedule that follows the pattern of actual rainfall. Some of the canal and dike work is being undone in an effort to restore the swamp, and the state plans to buy and preserve about 300,000 acres of Everglades land.

Many Everglades animals are still in danger. Only 30 Florida panthers are thought to remain, and more are killed on highways than are born each year. But it's hoped that as the swamp returns to normal, the animals will return, and the Everglades will again be the wetlands paradise it once was.

COLOR THEM WHITE

A snow white peacock? A pink and white koala? Outside a toy store, you wouldn't expect to see such animals. But they exist. They are albinos—animals that, by a quirk of inheritance, are snowy white instead of the usual colors of their kind.

The normal colors of animals are produced by pigment cells in the skin, fur or feathers, and eyes. Pigments are substances that produce color. One animal differs from another in color depending on the amount and kind of pigment these cells contain.

Albinos are animals that can't produce any pigments. True albinos have pure white coats or feathers and pink eyes. The pinkish eye coloring doesn't come from pigment— the color comes from blood in small vessels near the surface of the eye.

An animal may also be partly albino: Color is lacking in just some parts of the body or the animal is extremely pale, but not pure white, all over. Not all white animals are albinos, however. White animals such as polar bears have pigment in their skin and eyes.

Koala

Whitetail deer

44

Peacock

An albino is an animal that's white when it shouldn't be—it's normally meant to be another color.

Why do some animals lack color? Sometimes illness or stress will make normally colored fur or feathers turn white. But true albinism is an inherited trait. That is, it is passed on from parents to offspring by the genes inside cells. The genes tell the pigment cells which and how much color to produce.

The genes work in pairs, so an animal can inherit the gene for albinism and still be normally colored—as long as it has another gene for color. But suppose this animal mates with an animal that is also carrying the gene for albinism. If one of their offspring inherits genes for albinism from each parent, it will be white.

Albinism is more common among some animals than others, but it can occur in any species. Besides the animals shown here, it has been found in catfish, lobsters, trout, frogs, turtles, giraffes, rhinoceroses, porcu-

Gorilla

Hedgehog

pines, squirrels, robins, parrots, and many other animals—including people. In fact, even plants can be albinos. But albino plants won't live past the sprouting stage if they lack the green pigment known as chlorophyll. Chlorophyll helps the plant make food, and without it the plant can't live.

Albino animals have troubles of their own. Their white or pale color makes them easy for predators to spot. In addition, their eyes are sensitive to light because they contain no pigment to act as a sunshade. They often have poor vision and may not see a predator in time to escape.

The fact that albinos face such high risks means that they are quite rare in the wild. But in captivity, people protect them. People have long been fascinated by albino animals. In earlier times, the Indians believed that albino deer and buffalo were sacred and shouldn't be hunted. With their pale beauty, albinos are truly rare and special creatures.

Iguana

Chinstrap penguin

The United States regained the prestigious America's Cup from Australia in a four-race sweep.

THE AMERICA'S CUP RACE

In 1851 the schooner *America* won a yacht race around England's Isle of Wight, and skipper John Cox Stevens carried home an ornate silver cup. The trophy was turned over to the New York Yacht Club, which declared it an international challenge cup. The trophy—and the challenge races—became known as the America's Cup.

Over a period of 132 years, U.S. yachtsmen successfully defended the America's Cup against 24 foreign challenges, and the trophy remained firmly in the hands of the New York Yacht Club. But in September,

1983, the U.S. winning streak came to a stunning halt. In the waters off Newport, Rhode Island, a sleek challenger called *Australia II* swept past the American defender, *Liberty,* in four out of seven races. The America's Cup was removed from its case at the New York Yacht Club and carried away by the jubilant Australians.

In early 1987, off the coast of Fremantle, Western Australia, the America's Cup went up for grabs once again. The Australians wanted desperately to keep the trophy. The Americans wanted just as desperately to win it back. Teams from a number of other countries—including New Zealand, Canada, and France—also took aim at the prize. The outcome was a victory for the Americans, who prevailed after a hard-fought contest.

SETTING SAIL

The yachts that compete in the America's Cup are of the 12-meter class, a designation that refers not to the boat's length but to a formula based on length, width, sail area, and other factors. Every three or four years, the country in possession of the Cup defends its claim against the top challenger. The final competition is preceded by several months of qualifying rounds. Yachts from the host country compete in a series of races to determine which one will defend the Cup. Meanwhile, the other countries hold a round-robin elimination to determine the final challenger. In October, 1986, a total of thirteen yachts set sail in quest of the America's Cup. Each entry represented years of intensive preparation and millions of dollars in investment.

In the Australian camp, six yachts vied for the right to defend the Cup. Among the entries was a group headed by Alan Bond, whose *Australia II* had won the Cup in 1983. To the surprise of many, however, Bond's new yacht, *Australia IV,* was defeated in the qualifying round by a speedy entry called *Kookaburra III.* (A kookaburra is a large Australian bird with a loud cry.) The aluminum boat represented the Royal Perth Yacht Club, and it was skippered by 28-year-old Iain Murray.

Among the international challengers, *New Zealand* appeared to be the most formidable entry. In reaching the finals of the qualifying round, *New Zealand* compiled a record of 37 victories and only 1 defeat. Opposing *New Zealand* for the right to challenge *Kookaburra III* was an American entry, *Stars & Stripes,* of the San Diego Yacht Club. At the helm of *Stars & Stripes* was Dennis Conner, the skipper who had lost the America's Cup in 1983. Again to the surprise of many, *Stars & Stripes* defeated *New Zealand* in four out of five races. The United States had earned a chance to win back the Cup.

THE RACE IS ON

The course in America's Cup competition is 24.3 miles long, with a total of eight legs.

Prior to the final match series, *Stars & Stripes* was considered the faster yacht, but *Kookaburra III* was considered more maneuverable. The Americans were expected to have an advantage in strong winds, where the premium is on speed. (The sea winds off the coast of Western Australia were known to be generally strong and shifting.) The Aussies were expected to have an advantage in lighter winds, where the premium is on fast tacking (turning).

The first race in the best-of-seven series, held on January 31, proved the experts wrong. Sea winds were mostly light, but Conner and his ten-man crew maneuvered *Stars & Stripes* with clockwork precision. The challengers cruised home with a victory margin of 1 minute, 41 seconds.

The following day, the winds picked up, *Kookaburra III* squeaked out an early lead, but *Stars & Stripes* rushed back quickly. The Americans built steadily on their margin and crossed the finish line 1 minute, 10 seconds ahead of the Aussies. The challengers led 2–0 but refused to be overconfident.

With weather forecasters calling for light and variable breezes, the Australians were anxious to get the third race under way. *Kookaburra III* managed another early lead, but *Stars & Stripes* jumped back with some brilliant tactics and skillful maneuvering. Then the breeze freshened, and the Americans sped away to a 1 minute, 46 second victory. Still they refused to count their chickens. After all, *Liberty* had led 3–1 in 1983 and lost the Cup.

After a one-day layoff, the series resumed on February 4. If there had been any doubts as to which was the faster yacht, the answer came once and for all in the fourth race. *Kookaburra III* employed aggressive tactics from the outset, but *Stars & Stripes* sailed a flawless race and led every step of the way. The Americans won by a whopping 1 minute, 59 seconds, completing a 4–0 sweep of the 1987 challenge series.

And so, just as in 1851, the ornate silver trophy was carried off to the United States. Even as it went on display at the San Diego Yacht Club, however, potential challengers from around the world were planning for the next America's Cup series.

JEFFREY H. HACKER
Editor, *The Olympic Story*

DINOSAUR DAYS

For 165 million years, dinosaurs ruled the Earth. The ground trembled under the tread of these giant beasts. Then, 65 million years ago, they died out, leaving only fossilized remains as clues to their existence. But that hasn't kept dinosaurs from being a hot topic.

People have long been fascinated by these huge creatures and the riddles they pose. What sort of animals were they? How did they behave when they roamed the Earth? What, exactly, did they look like? And above all, what caused them to die out?

In recent years, paleontologists (scientists who study the fossils of Earth's early creatures) have made startling new discoveries. Their finds have given rise to new theories about dinosaurs and new answers to the questions about them.

WARM-BLOODED, WARM-HEARTED?

The first scientists to piece together the fossilized bones of dinosaurs found that the creatures looked like giant lizards. (In fact, the name "dinosaur" comes from Greek words meaning "terrible lizard.") Thus they assumed that, like present-day lizards and other reptiles, dinosaurs were cold-blooded. The body temperatures of cold-blooded animals fluctuate with the temperature of the air. Warm-blooded animals such as birds and mammals maintain a constant body temperature regardless of the outside air.

Because cold-blooded animals are generally slow-moving, scientists assumed that dinosaurs were sluggish and clumsy. That assumption led to some theories about why they vanished: Perhaps the slow-moving dinosaurs simply couldn't compete with faster-moving mammals and so died out. Or perhaps the Earth's temperature changed and became too cold for them.

Now new studies of dinosaur fossils—including fossilized tracks—show that many dinosaurs weren't slow-moving at all. Many

Based on new discoveries about dinosaurs, scientists now think that the extinct creatures were sleek and active, stood upright on their hind legs and carried their tails in the air, cared for their young, and may even have been brightly colored.

were sleek and agile. Some, it appears, could zip along as fast as 30 miles (48 kilometers) an hour. Many dinosaurs also seem to have stood upright on their hind legs, rather than hugging the ground as modern reptiles do. That meant that their circulatory systems had to have a high enough blood pressure to pump blood up to their heads—a trait of warm-blooded animals.

Dinosaurs seem to have had other warm-blooded traits. Most reptiles don't pay attention to their young. But recently, scientists have found nesting sites that suggest that some dinosaurs cared for their offspring much as birds do.

As an example, the scientists point to duck-billed dinosaurs called *Maiasaurs* (the name means "good mother lizard"). *Maiasaurs* lived in the lowlands of what is now Montana some 80 million years ago. But fossils show that they migrated to higher ground to build nests, lay eggs, and raise their young. The nests were grouped in colonies, like those of many birds. And the parent dinosaurs seem to have brought food—berries and grasses—to the hatchlings for several months, until they were large enough to leave the nests and find their own food.

Many dinosaurs also seem to have traveled in vast herds, with older dinosaurs protecting the young ones. And unlike cold-blooded creatures, young dinosaurs grew fast. Newborn *Maiasaurs* were about a foot (30 centimeters) long at birth and grew as much as 10 feet (3 meters) in their first year of life. A rapid growth rate requires a rapid metabolism—yet another trait of warm-blooded animals. ("Metabolism" refers to all the chemical changes that take place in a plant or animal to keep it alive.)

These and other traits suggest that at least some dinosaurs were warm-blooded. Some scientists even think that certain dinosaurs may have been the ancestors of modern birds. Their theory is supported by fossils of dinosaurs with birdlike bone structures.

MORE DINOSAUR NEWS

Scientists have made other new discoveries about dinosaurs. For example, most people think of dinosaurs as enormous—and many were. The largest dinosaur found so far—dubbed Ultrasaurus and a member of the genus *Brachiosaurus*—was about 60 feet (18 meters) tall and weighed about 80 tons. But in 1986, scientists in Nova Scotia, Canada, found footprints of a dinosaur that was no bigger than a sparrow.

More than 50 new kinds of dinosaurs have been found since 1970. Among the finds was one of the oldest dinosaur skeletons on record, discovered in Arizona in 1985. Nicknamed Dinosaur Gertie, this creature was about the size of an ostrich and lived 225 million years ago.

Dinosaur bones have now been found in all regions of the world, from the Arctic to Antarctica. This supports the theory that the continents were connected in the days of the dinosaurs and later broke apart and moved to their present locations. For example, North America was once linked to Asia, and scientists think herds of dinosaurs migrated between China and Canada.

There are also new ideas about what dinosaurs looked like. Some scientists think that dinosaurs may have been brightly colored, as birds and lizards are today. Rather than dragging their tails on the ground, they may have carried them in the air and used them for balance.

A few years ago, scientists learned that skeletons of *Brontosaurus* had been fitted with the wrong heads—these huge planteating creatures had longer, more tapered heads than had been supposed. Now researchers have given a new look to another familiar dinosaur, *Stegosaurus*. For years, this creature was portrayed with a double row of armor plates sticking up from its back. But a study of *Stegosaurus* fossils has shown that there was only one row of armor plates. Some scientists think the animal could move the plates up and down with its back muscles and may have used them to protect itself from attack or to absorb heat from the sun.

Another study has laid to rest a controversy over whether humans and dinosaurs could have lived at the same time. Most scientists have long believed that the last dinosaurs died out more than 60 million years before the first ancestors of humans appeared. But fossils along the Paluxy River in Texas seemed to show human tracks mingled with dinosaur tracks.

Finally, in 1986, scientists were able to explain the confusing evidence. Most of the tracks in the riverbed were made by dinosaurs that walked on their three toes, as dinosaurs usually did. The ones that looked like human tracks were made by dinosaurs that placed their feet full on the ground. The faint toe marks had been overlooked.

WHY DID DINOSAURS DIE OUT?

The new information about dinosaurs has given rise to new theories about how and why they died out. Scientists no longer blame some defect in dinosaurs themselves, such as the inability to move quickly or maintain their body temperatures. Instead, the evidence points to a worldwide catastrophe: At the time that dinosaurs became extinct, some 70 percent of the world's plant and animal species also died out.

What could have caused such drastic changes? One theory is that the climate turned colder, killing off many plant species. Since many animals depend on plants for food, they died too. Another theory is that changes in Earth's magnetic field allowed increased amounts of deadly radiation from space to reach Earth. Or perhaps the atmosphere changed—in 1987, scientists tested air trapped in samples of amber that were 80 million years old and found it was vastly richer in oxygen than present-day air.

One popular theory blames a freak event:

For many years it was believed that *Stegosaurus* had a double row of armor plates sticking up from its back *(left)*. But fossils have shown that the dinosaur had only one row of armor plates *(above)*.

DELIGHTED WITH DINOSAURS

In 1987 dinosaurs were bigger than ever—not in size, but in popularity. Dinosaurs were hot, especially with kids. Museums dusted off their dinosaur bones and staged special exhibits. Several hosted a touring show of dinosaur art. And dinosaur toys were among the top sellers of the year. There were dinosaur dolls, model dinosaur skeletons, dinosaur coloring books, and dinosaur clocks. Dinosaurs appeared in games and puzzles and on T-shirts. There were even dinosaur-shaped pasta pieces —called, of course, Spaghettisaurus.

Why the sudden boom in dinosaurs? New discoveries about the giant creatures probably had something to do with it—dinosaurs were in the news. But as with other fads of recent years, no one was sure how this wave of popularity had evolved—or when it would become extinct!

the crash of a huge asteroid on Earth. According to this theory, the asteroid would have caused earthquakes and tidal waves. It also would have thrown up enough dust to fill the atmosphere for years, blocking the light of the sun. Without sunlight, first plants and then animals would have died. But some living things—such as plants that produced seeds that would lie dormant until the light returned and animals that could hibernate—would have survived.

Scientists who accept this theory point to high concentrations of an element called iridium in sediments that were laid down 65 million years ago. Iridium is rare on the Earth's surface but more common in asteroids. Some scientists note that iridium is present in the Earth's core and could have been thrown up in volcanic eruptions. But the same layers of sediment that contain iridium also contain fractured quartz crystals. The fractures are evidence of a sudden, powerful impact—such as might have been caused by an asteroid.

If a giant asteroid collided with Earth 65 million years ago, it would have left a vast crater. Yet no such crater produced that long ago has been found. Scientists who support the asteroid theory think the crater may have originally been on the ocean floor and was wiped out as the continents shifted over millions of years. In 1987 a discovery was made that lent support to this theory. On the ocean floor off Nova Scotia, scientists found the remains of a huge crater formed by the impact of a comet or asteroid. The crater was thought to be about 50 million years old. The scientists hoped that by studying it, they would learn more about the effects of asteroid collisions.

But the asteroid theory isn't accepted by all scientists, and many questions remain. For example, some fossil evidence suggests that dinosaurs were already on the decline by the time the catastrophic event—whatever it was—took place. Many of the other species that died out around that time also seem to have disappeared gradually. It may be that, if the asteroid crash took place, it was just one of many events in a complex series of changes that brought the days of the dinosaurs to a close.

FAN-FARE

Hand-held fans have a practical purpose: On a hot day or in a stuffy room, they create a cooling breeze. But throughout their long history, fans have been far more than useful objects.

Delicate and richly decorated, these accessories have been symbols of rank and aristocracy and "musts" for fashionable women. Special fans have been created to commemorate important events and even to advertise products. And today, when air conditioning has replaced the fan as the most common cooling device, beautiful fans are valued as works of art.

FAN HISTORY

People may have used fans before the dawn of history—the first ones were probably large leaves or palm fronds. They were followed by fans made of ostrich plumes and other feathers. Such fans were used in ceremonies and by royalty in many ancient civilizations. But the Chinese may have been the first to have fans for ordinary use, perhaps as early as 2000 B.C. These fans were carried by both men and women.

Early Chinese fans were handscreens—flat, rigid boards—made of wood, woven rushes, and paper or embroidered fabrics stretched over wooden frames. Handles were formed of ivory, jade, gold, silver, laquered wood, and other materials. These fans came in many shapes, including heart-shaped, moon-shaped, and pear-shaped. The Chinese are also thought to have been the first to paint designs on fans.

In the 600's A.D., the Japanese invented the folding fan, formed of flat sticks riveted together at one end. Folding fans were far less bulky than handscreens, and their popularity quickly spread. Again, all sorts of materials were used. There were even iron-ribbed fans that warriors could carry into battle. This wasn't as silly as it sounds—not only did these battle fans make good weapons, the Japanese commanders also used them to send signals to their troops.

Off the battlefield, Chinese and Japanese court etiquette dictated how fans should be held and used. For example, high-ranking Chinese officials who passed each other on the street were allowed to cover their faces with their fans. That way, they wouldn't have to acknowledge each other and go through elaborate rituals of greeting. Etiquette also decreed that fans should be used only in warm weather, and certain types of fans were reserved for the hottest days. Fans were often presented as gifts, to show esteem and goodwill.

Fans have an ancient history in Western countries, too. Bearers carrying long-handled ostrich-plume fans attended the rulers of ancient Egypt. Feather fans were also used in ancient Greece and Rome, and women of that time often carried hand-screens. Our word "fan" comes from the Latin word *vannus,* the name of a flat, fan-like tool used in winnowing grain.

Fans were an important part of Greek and Roman religious rituals, and the early Christian church used them in its ceremonies. In Medieval Europe, court ladies (and sometimes men) carried flag-shaped leather hand-screens or cockades—folding fans that opened to a full circle, with end sticks that formed a long handle. Fans made from peacock, ostrich, and parakeet feathers, with jewel-studded handles of ivory and silver, were popular in the 1400's and 1500's.

As European explorers began to roam the world's oceans at about this time, they brought back many strange items. Among them were folding fans from China and Japan. Europeans were quick to adopt this new fashion, first in Italy and then in France and other countries. Although handscreens and cockades remained in use, folding fans soon became the most popular type.

Royalty and the nobility were the primary users of fans at this time. Queen Elizabeth I of England was said to have been especially fond of them. From the early 1600's on, however, the fan more and more became an accessory that no well-dressed, sophisticated woman could do without. European craftsmen turned out thousands of fans each year, and thousands more were imported from China.

By the end of the 1700's, men had stopped carrying fans. But women used fans to shield their faces from the heat of open fireplaces in winter. In summer, fluttering fans cooled them and shooed away insects and unpleasant odors. A fashionable woman needed several fans—everyday fans, fancy-dress fans,

Ivory brisé fan, China, mid-1800's

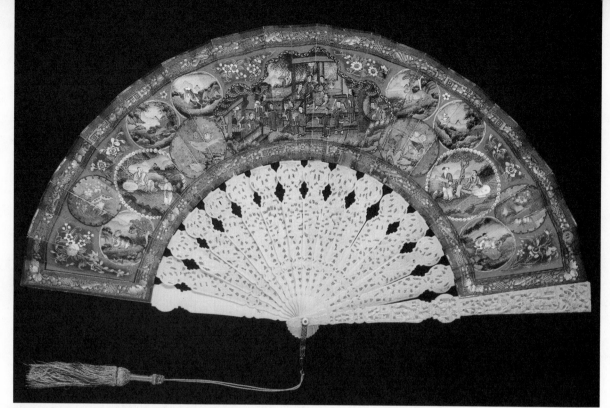

Ivory and silk pleated fan, China, mid-1800's

fans to go with different outfits. And special fans were made for special occasions. Bridal fans—made of ivory, satin, and lace and carrying pictures of Cupid, hearts, and other symbols of love—were given by grooms to their brides. A woman who was in mourning might carry a black or gray fan, with discreet decorations.

A fan was more than a useful accessory—it was a mark of grace and style. Etiquette manuals gave instructions on proper fan use. "Even the most charming and elegant woman, if she cannot manage her fan, appears ridiculous," cautioned one author.

The way a woman held and used her fan even became a method of communication. It was said that in the "language of fans," different motions had meanings. When a

Tortoise shell, silk, and ostrich feather pleated fan, United States, 1920's

Ivory and silk pleated fan, Western Europe, mid-1800's

woman held her open fan by her left ear, for example, she was saying, "Do not betray our secret." A half-open fan pressed to the lips meant, "You may kiss me." Historians doubt that such set meanings were ever really used. But there is no question that a woman could communicate many things by the way she snapped, fluttered, and carried her fan.

FABULOUS FOLDING FANS

There are two basic types of folding fans, the *brisé* fan and the pleated fan. *Brisé* is the French word for "broken" or "collapsible." This type of fan is formed of wide, flat sticks that fold up between decorative end pieces (called guards). A rivet fastens them together at the base of the fan. At the top, a ribbon links them so that they overlap slightly when

Ivory and parchment pleated fan, France, mid-1700's

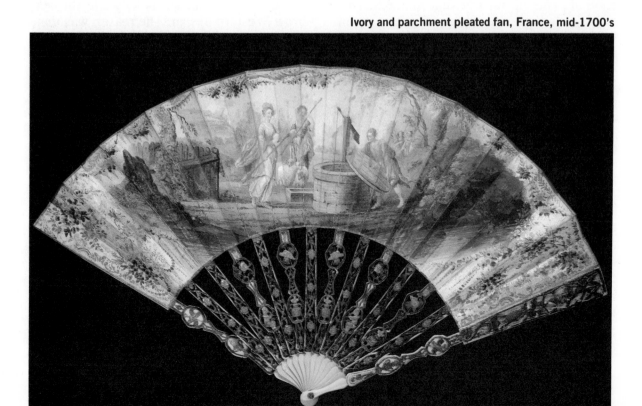

Ivory and silk cockade fan, United States, mid-1800's

the fan is open. In a pleated fan, the upper parts of the flat sticks support a semicircular band of paper or other flexible material. This band, called the leaf, is pleated so that it will fold up neatly between the guards when the fan is closed.

Both methods of construction are clever. But the materials and decoration that have been used are what make folding fans truly delightful. Sticks and guards have been made of ivory, bone, mother-of-pearl, horn, tortoiseshell, metal, and wood, including bamboo and fragrant sandalwood. They have been carved, painted, gilded, lacquered, pierced to look like lace, and studded with metal pins, spangles, and gems.

The leaves of pleated fans have been made of parchment, lace, silk, linen, and other fine fabrics, as well as of paper. Like the sticks, the leaves have been pierced, painted with all kinds of scenes and designs, and decorated with spangles, feathers, tiny pearls,

and pieces of ivory and mica. Modern fans are often made of plastics and other synthetics that mimic these finer materials.

Like other articles of fashion, fans have been subject to fads and whims in East and West alike. The pictures and designs painted on them generally reflected the styles of art popular at the time they were made. Chinese and Japanese fans, for example, were made in many different styles and often carried short messages or poems in delicate calligraphy. The paintings were considered works of art, and the artists signed them. Sometimes the leaves of pleated fans would be removed from their frames and collected in albums.

Like other Chinese and Japanese paintings, these fan paintings often showed birds, flowers, and scenes from nature, delicately rendered in simple brushstrokes. Silk and paper with a gold or silver sheen were popular background materials. Bright red paper with gold designs was used in fans designed for special occasions like birthdays and New Year celebrations. In China, black was a color once reserved for the lower classes, but in the late 1800's black fans with gold and silver decorations became popular even with the aristocracy.

During their heyday in the West, fans likewise had many styles of decoration. Chinese designs were always popular because they suited the folding fan's origin in Asia. Sometimes the sticks and guards of a pleated fan would have a Chinese look, while the leaf bore a Western design. The reason was that, especially in the 1700's, sticks and guards were often imported from China and fitted with leaves when they arrived. Scenes from classical, Biblical, and mythological tales were also very popular in the 1700's, and fans of this time often carried miniature copies of famous paintings.

In the mid-1800's, the Victorians turned from painted scenes to elaborately carved and decorated sticks, painted designs, and exotic materials such as satin, lace, sequins, and feathers. But after new trade links were opened between Japan and the West in the 1860's, Japanese designs enjoyed a wave of popularity. And around the turn of the century, fans reflected the art nouveau style, with swirling, free designs based on peacocks, flowers, and other natural forms.

While most fans were designed to look elegant and made use of rich materials, some were designed to deliver a message. For example, after the French Revolution, the French currency collapsed, and people began to carry fans papered with worthless bank notes and IOU's. And from the late 1700's on, printed fans were very popular.

Some printed fans were aids to memory—they carried rules for card games, dance steps, the words and music of songs, historical information, and maps. Church and chapel fans had prayers and psalms. Children's fans—smaller than adults' fans—carried the alphabet.

Other special fans were made to commemorate important events, such as the first balloon flight, in 1783. Travelers brought back souvenir fans that showed scenes of the places they visited. And as time went on, advertisers got into the game. Fans carried messages that plugged everything from hotels to cologne. Because these fans were designed to be given away, they were often cheaply made, with plain wooden (or, later, celluloid) sticks and thin paper leaves. But many had lovely designs.

Some fans were conversation pieces, with riddles or cartoons that poked fun at the society or the politics of the times. Another type of fan that was sure to spark comment was the autograph fan—a plain white fan that could be "decorated" with the signatures of friends and famous people.

Telescope fans became popular in the 1800's. These fans had telescoping sticks that could be shortened, so that the folded fan could be tucked in a small handbag. And at one time or another, many other gimmicks were added to fans.

Trick and puzzle fans were two special types of *brisé* fans. A trick fan looked like any other *brisé* fan—as long as it was opened from left to right. If your friend tried to open it from right to left, it would appear to fall apart, as though the ribbon holding the tops of the sticks had broken. Puzzle fans showed four different pictures: one on each side when opened from right to left, and two more when opened from left to right.

Domino and mask fans had eyeholes, so that the bearer could hide her face and peer out. Lorgnette fans featured a small magnifying glass, usually set in one of the guards.

The French queen Marie Antoinette, who was nearsighted, had one of these fans. And in the late 1800's, all kinds of odd fans were invented—pistol fans, parasol fans, fans made of rubber.

By World War I, however, fans were falling out of fashion in Western countries. Women were becoming more emancipated and didn't need to hide behind their fans. Clothing was more comfortable, and houses could be cooled with electrical fans.

Flashy ostrich-plume fans made a brief comeback in the 1930's, as accessories for evening gowns. But by this time, fans no longer served a useful purpose, and they were gradually set aside. Today the delicate and lovely fans of the past can be seen in museums and private collections, where they stand as reminders of the elegance of the past.

Painted cardboard handscreen, France, late 1800's

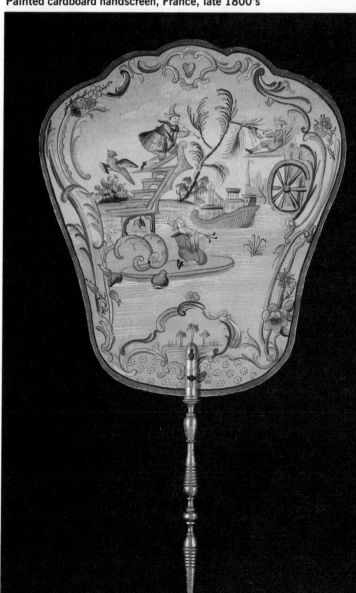

The Wind Lion

The autumn sun filtered through the forest, splashing across the path where Bambi, the fawn, and his rabbit friend, Thumper, stood. They were watching the animals get ready for winter.

Squirrels raced to their dens in the trees with cheeks stuffed full of acorns.

Dirt flew from the groundhog's hole as he made it deeper and lined it with soft grasses. It would be a warm and cozy place for him to sleep when the weather grew cold.

Bambi and Thumper watched the dark vee-shapes of geese and ducks flying in formation across the cold, pale autumn sky.

"When the vees go in the other direction," said Thumper, "that will mean it's spring."

But Bambi didn't say anything. He was watching one of the flocks.

"Look up there, Thumper," he said. "Do you see that dark spot flying by itself? It just left the flock. And it looks like it's headed for our pond."

"Let's go!" cried Thumper, and the two friends raced off to the pond.

They arrived in time to see a large Canada goose, wings outstretched, land feet first in the pond. It arched its beautiful black neck over its body and glided slowly across the water to the thick clumps of rushes that grew on the far side of the pond. It nibbled at them for a bit and then waddled onto shore, dragging a limp wing behind it.

Thumper and Bambi were there to greet the bird.

"What's wrong with your wing?" Thumper blurted out. "Did you hurt it? We saw you in the sky. Are you gonna stay here?"

"Hooooold on, little rabbit," said the goose in a tired voice. "I need some rest." And he nestled down under some shrubs near the water, tucked his head under his wing, and was snoring softly before Thumper could fire off another round of questions.

"I guess we'll have to wait until he wakes up to find out who he is," said Bambi. "C'mon, Thumper. Let's go back and see how the squirrels are getting along."

When the goose finally opened his eyes, Bambi and Thumper were the first things he saw. Thumper peppered him with questions. And the goose answered them. He told how he had flown at the tip of the vee-formation during a storm, breaking the way for the rest of the flock. His wing had begun to ache later, and he'd flown down to rest before continuing the long journey south.

"Storms scare me," said Thumper. "They scare Bambi, too," Bambi nodded shyly. It was hard to admit to the brave goose that he was frightened of anything.

In the days that followed, Bambi and Thumper spent many hours at the pond's edge listening to the goose tell stories.

He told them what it was like to fly. He told them about his home on the big lakes in Canada. But the story they liked best was the one about the wind lion.

"The wind lion lives deep in the Canadian forests where it is rarely seen," began the goose, telling the story for probably the fifth time. "It has the head, feet, and tail of a lion. It has the body of a giant eagle, and large, powerful wings that you can hear beating a mile away. It sounds like this." The goose spread out his own massive wings

and beat the air slowly, making a whooshing sound. "And when the wind lion gets angry, it roars like thunder."

"How do you make a wind lion angry?" asked Thumper in a small voice.

"By asking too many questions," chuckled the goose. "Now remember," he added, seeing the scared look on the little rabbit's face. "There's only one way to get rid of a wind lion once you've made one angry. You have to look straight into its eyes, gather all your strength and . . ." the goose paused for effect.

"And do what?" begged Thumper.

"Tell him to go away," said the goose, winking playfully.

The sun was slowly sinking behind the mountain ridge, and it was just light enough to see black rain clouds edging across the evening sky when the goose finally finished the story. A chilly autumn wind brushed

"I think so," said Bambi, "but just to be sure, maybe you'd better not ask any more questions."

"Maybe we should stay here until the storm passes," said Thumper, trying to sound brave. Bambi agreed. They both knew it wasn't safe to be out in a storm.

Soon the sounds of the storm died away, and in the quiet that followed, the two friends listened for danger before leaving the safety of the thicket.

Thumper's sharp ears were the first to hear the noise. Then Bambi heard it too. It was the sound of powerful wingbeats flying through the dark, dripping forest. *Whooosh, whooosh, whooosh!* The sound was low to the ground and very close.

"It's the wind lion!" sobbed Thumper.

Then the sound was gone. Bambi and Thumper strained as they listened for more sounds in the dark.

"Here it comes again!" cried Thumper. He buried his head under his paws.

past them, making the goose ruffle his feathers for warmth and sending a chill through Thumper and Bambi.

"It smells like rain," said Bambi. "We'd better go home." They had stayed much too late.

"Don't forget," called the goose. "The wind lion is just a story."

"I know," said Thumper, but he was finding it hard not to believe the wind lion was real.

As they made their way home, the trees began to take on strange shapes in the darkening forest. The wind began to blow harder, stirring the branches and making a spooky whistling sound. The two friends hurried along as drops of rain began to splash down.

A low rumbling sound sent them diving into a nearby thicket.

"Do you think that rumbling sound is thunder?" asked Thumper, thinking about what the wind lion sounded like when it roared.

Whoooosh, whoooosh, whoooosh! Closer and closer came the sound of the powerful wingbeats. They were just overhead when Bambi gathered all his nerve and leaped out into the forest path. Looking up, he saw a large winged shape flying above him and he yelled at it with all his might: "Go away, wind lion!"

"Bambi, is that you?" called the familiar voice of his friend, the goose. Bambi heaved a sigh of relief as the goose—and not the wind lion—landed in front of him.

"I was worried about you," the goose said. "I came to see if you made it home all right."

Thumper stuck his nose out of the thicket. "We were hiding from the wind lion," he said. "You must have scared him away."

The goose laughed. "No, no, I believe I am your wind lion. Or what you thought was one. I've been flying back and forth looking for you. Come, I'll help you get home."

Bambi and Thumper were happy to have their friend take them home. And their mothers were happy to see them safe and sound after the big storm.

The next morning, a bright autumn sun shone warmly on the damp forest as Bambi and Thumper raced along the path toward the pond. But when they got to the goose's resting place, it was empty.

"He's gone," said Bambi. "I can't believe he just left."

"He didn't even say good-bye," said Thumper angrily.

Later Bambi and his mother talked about the goose.

"It's not that he didn't care about you, Bambi," she said, nuzzling the top of his head. "It's just that it's a natural thing for the goose to continue south. That instinct is stronger than friendship."

"But I never got a chance to tell him how much I liked him," said Bambi.

"I'm sure he knew that," said his mother.

"And I wanted something to remember him by," said Bambi.

"You do have something," she said. "Every time you're scared, you can think of your friend the goose who helped you overcome your fears by learning to face them."

"At least I'd like to be able to thank him for that," said Bambi.

"Your friendship was thanks enough," said his mother.

Bambi knew she was right, but he couldn't help feeling a little sad every time he saw the empty place near the thick clumps of rushes on the far side of the pond.

SEASONS OF SPICE

In spring, many trees are covered with pink blossoms. As the blossoms die, green leaves open, covering the trees through the warm days of summer. The leaves turn to shades of yellow and red in autumn, then fall to the ground. In winter, the trees' brown branches are exposed to view.

Using dried herbs and spices, you can make a wall hanging that re-creates this passing of the four seasons. Use sesame seeds or onion flakes for the blossoms of spring (you can give them a pink tone with watercolors or a felt-tip marker). For the leaves of summer, use a bright green herb such as parsley or chives. Crushed red pepper can represent autumn's colorful foliage. Cloves form the branches of winter. Pieces of cinnamon stick make the tree trunks.

Begin by deciding on the size and shape of the hanging. You may want to make a vertical arrangement, such as the one shown here. But horizontal and square arrangements are attractive too.

Next choose the background. Fabrics such as burlap and felt work well for vertical wallhangings. Wood or heavy cardboard can be used for arrangements of any shape. Heavy cardboard set inside a picture frame is a good choice for a square arrangement.

If the wallhanging is made of burlap, pull out a few of the vertical threads on both sides to create frayed edges. Then turn under the top and bottom edges and glue them in place.

On scrap paper, draw a model tree, cut it out and make three copies. Place these on the background to be certain that they can be evenly arranged on the material. Lightly trace around them.

Use white glue to attach the herbs and spices to the background. After the glue has dried, you might add a second and even a third layer to some of the treetops. This will increase the three-dimensional look. You can also add "grass" around the bases of the trunks, using tarragon or rosemary. Color the spring treetop after all the layers have been added and the glue has dried. Be gentle, or the "blossoms" will fall off!

Find a special spot in your home where you can display the four spicy seasons.

A SEEDY PICTURE

You don't need paints to create a painting. Instead, use beans to express your artistic talents. A walk through a supermarket will show you that dried beans come in a wide variety of colors: red kidney beans, brown lentils, green and yellow split peas, speckled pintos, and much more. There is great variety in shape and size, too, which will give your bean "painting" interesting textures.

Begin by getting an appropriate piece of wood, perhaps a piece of lumber or even a kitchen cutting board. Sketch your picture onto the wood. You can also use a picture from a book or magazine and trace it onto the wood. Decide which beans have the best colors, shapes, and sizes for your design, and arrange them on the picture. Then glue the beans to the wood using white glue. When the glue has dried, cover the picture with several coats of polyurethane to preserve the beans.

Enclose your bean picture in a natural or painted wood frame. Or create the frame shown above—a border of rope and several rows of dark beans.

Basil Rathbone strikes a familiar pose in one of his sixteen film portrayals of the great Sherlock Holmes.

SHERLOCK HOLMES— STILL ALIVE AT 100

"Mr. Holmes thanks you for your letter. At the moment he is in retirement in Sussex, keeping bees."

Every week, dozens of letters addressed to "Mr. Sherlock Holmes" are mailed to 221B Baker Street in London, the fictional residence of the world's greatest detective. In the building where 221 would have stood, the occupants send out gracious replies, informing correspondents that the celebrated sleuth has retired to his favorite hobby.

Tall and lean, dressed in a deerstalker hat and Inverness cape, smoking a pipe, and peering through a magnifying glass, Sherlock Holmes is one of the most familiar figures in all of literature. Certainly no other fictional character has been mistaken more often for a real person. In 1987, 100 years after his literary debut, Holmes was still being celebrated by hero-worshippers around the world.

The character of Sherlock Holmes—with his faithful friend, Dr. Watson—was the creation of the British writer Sir Arthur Conan Doyle. The brilliant private detective was introduced in a short novel, *A Study in Scarlet,* published in 1887. Before retiring to Sussex, Holmes appeared in a total of four novels and fifty-six short stories. Over the decades, millions of readers—in 57 different languages—have followed Holmes' adventures and delighted in his ability to solve the most baffling mysteries.

CONAN DOYLE—AUTHOR AND ADVENTURER

Sir Arthur Conan Doyle, creator of the master detective, was born on May 22, 1859, in Edinburgh, Scotland. As a young boy he loved to read adventure tales, and he wrote stories of his own. After studying at Jesuit schools in England and Austria, he entered the University of Edinburgh and received a bachelor of medicine degree in 1881.

Graduation from medical school brought adventure for Conan Doyle. First he spent seven months as ship's surgeon on a whaler bound for the Arctic. Then, upon his return, he signed up for a voyage to West Africa. His experiences on those journeys had a major influence on the rest of his life—and on his writings.

In 1882, after returning from Africa, Conan Doyle set up a medical practice in Southsea, England. Patients were scarce, however, and so the young doctor took to writing. He managed to sell a few adventure stories, but they earned him very little money.

The year 1885 marked a turning point in Conan Doyle's life. That summer he was awarded his doctor of medicine degree from the University of Edinburgh. A few weeks later he was married to Louise Hawkins. And it is believed to be the year in which he conceived the character that would become one of the most popular in all of literature.

INTRODUCING SHERLOCK HOLMES

How was Sherlock Holmes "born"? Where did the idea come from?

Having decided to write a detective novel, Conan Doyle began to think about a main character. His mind drifted back to medical school, and he remembered a professor named Dr. Joseph Bell. Bell was a tall, thin man with a prominent nose and sharp, penetrating gray eyes. A professor of surgery, Bell constantly urged his students to develop their powers of observation. Gather facts carefully, he taught, then examine them closely and put them together to form logical conclusions. It was precisely these skills—keen scientific observation and brilliant deductive reasoning—that Conan Doyle gave to his detective.

When Conan Doyle began writing *A Study in Scarlet,* he named his sleuth "Sherrinford Holmes" (after the American author Oliver Wendell Holmes). For the good Dr. Watson, he originally thought of "Ormond Sacker." One wonders how successful the stories would have been if he had kept those names.

Like most of the other Sherlock Holmes stories, *A Study in Scarlet* is told in the words of Dr. Watson. It is in this book that Watson meets the great detective for the first time:

"Dr. Watson, Mr. Sherlock Holmes," said Stamford, introducing us.

"How are you?" he said cordially, grip- *ping my hand with a strength for which I should hardly have given him credit. "You have been in Afghanistan, I perceive."*

"How on earth did you know that?" I asked in astonishment.

Intriguing as the character of Sherlock Holmes was, Conan Doyle's creation wasn't an immediate success. A number of publishers rejected *A Study in Scarlet* before it finally appeared in 1887 in a British magazine called *Beeton's Christmas Annual.* But even then it didn't catch on, and Conan Doyle thought of giving up his character.

A break came in 1888, when an American publisher asked Conan Doyle to do another Sherlock Holmes novel. It was this second story, *The Sign of Four,* that launched Holmes and Watson to international fame. A few years later, Conan Doyle left medicine to write full-time.

THE LEGEND GROWS

The first Holmes short story, "A Scandal in Bohemia," was published in the *Strand Magazine* in July, 1891. Many others followed. With each adventure the great detective won new admirers, and Conan Doyle

A STUDY IN SCARLET

An American named Enoch J. Drebber is found dead in an empty house at 3 Lauriston Gardens, London. There is no evidence as to how the man met his death, and the two Scotland Yard detectives assigned to the case, Lestrade and Gregson, are baffled. For help, they call on Sherlock Holmes.

The case is called *A Study in Scarlet,* the first of 60 mysteries to which the great Sherlock Holmes applies his remarkable powers of observation and deduction. As ever, the story is told by Holmes' loyal companion, Dr. John H. Watson.

The investigation begins upon Holmes' arrival at 3 Lauriston Gardens. After examining the grounds in front of the house, the keen-eyed sleuth moves inside to the dining room—the scene of the apparent crime . . .

Sherlock Holmes approached the body, and, kneeling down, examined it intently. "You are sure that there is no wound?" he asked, pointing to numerous splashes of blood which lay all round.

"Positive!" cried both detectives.

"Then, of course, this blood belongs to a second individual—presumably the murderer, if murder has been committed. . . ."

As he spoke, his nimble fingers were flying here, there, and everywhere, feeling, pressing, unbuttoning, examining, while his eyes wore the same far-away expression which I have already remarked upon. So swiftly was the examination made, that one would hardly have guessed the minuteness with which it was conducted. Finally, he sniffed the dead man's lips, and then glanced at the soles of his patent leather boots.

As Holmes ponders the case and discusses the evidence with Gregson, Detective Lestrade makes an eerie discovery. On the wall in a dark corner of the room, a single word has been scrawled in blood: "Rache." Detective Lestrade is triumphant. "You mark my words," he declares, "when this case comes to be cleared up, you will find that a woman named Rachel has something to do with it."

Holmes isn't so sure . . .

He whipped a tape measure and a large round magnifying glass from his pocket. With these two implements he trotted noiselessly about the room, sometimes stopping, occasionally kneeling, and once lying flat upon his face. So engrossed was he with his occupation that he appeared to have forgotten our presence, for he chattered away to himself under his breath the whole time, keeping up a running fire of exclamations, groans, whistles, and little cries suggestive of encouragement and of hope. As I watched him I was irresistibly reminded of a pure-blooded, well-trained foxhound as it dashes backwards and forwards through the covert, whining in its eagerness, until it comes across the lost scent. For twenty minutes or more he continued his researches, measuring with the most exact care the distance between marks which were entirely invisible to me, and occasionally applying his tape to the walls in an equally incomprehensible manner. In one place he gathered up very carefully a little pile of grey dust from the floor, and packed it away in an envelope. Finally he examined with his glass the word upon the wall, going over every letter of it with the most minute exactness. This done, he appeared to be satisfied, for he replaced his tape and his glass in his pocket.

"They say that genius is an infinite capacity for taking pains," he remarked with a smile. "It's a very bad definition, but it does apply to detective work. . . ."

"I'll tell you one thing which may help you in the case," he continued. "There has been murder done, and the murderer was a man. He was more than six feet high, was in the prime of life, had small feet for his height, wore coarse, square-toed boots and smoked a Trichinopoly cigar. He came here with his victim in a four-wheeled cab, which was drawn by a horse with three old shoes and one new one on his off fore-leg. In all probability the murderer had a florid face, and the finger-nails of his right hand were remarkably long. These are only a few indications, but they may assist you."

Lestrade and Gregson glanced at each other with an incredulous smile.

"If this man was murdered, how was it done?" asked the former.

"Poison," said Sherlock Holmes curtly, and strode off. "One other thing, Lestrade," he added, turning round at the door: " 'Rache' is the German word for 'revenge'; so don't lose your time looking for Miss Rachel."

With which parting shot he walked away, leaving the two rivals open-mouthed behind him.

earned greater fame and fortune. But by 1893, after two dozen stories, Conan Doyle grew tired of his character. He decided to kill him off. In a story called "The Final Problem," Holmes and his archenemy, Professor Moriarty, fall to their deaths over the Reichenbach Falls in Switzerland. Conan Doyle was overwhelmed with letters pleading with him to bring Holmes back to life. "Let's Keep Holmes Alive" clubs were started in several U.S. cities. Magazines offered huge sums of money for new stories.

Conan Doyle, meanwhile, had many other interests to pursue. He had a daughter, Mary Louise, and a son, Kingsley. (Later there would be three more children by a second marriage.) He was a lover of sports and outdoor life. He was active in British politics. He wrote "serious" historical novels. And in 1900, eager to witness the Boer War, he sailed for South Africa, where he ran a field hospital for British troops. His book about that conflict, *The Great Boer War* (1900), is still a standard historical reference. In 1902, Conan Doyle was knighted for his support of the British war effort. He became *Sir* Arthur Conan Doyle.

HOLMES LIVES!

All the while, pressure had continued to build for the return of Sherlock Holmes. Finally, Conan Doyle heeded the call. In 1902, after an eight-year absence, Holmes made his reappearance in a new novel, *The Hound of the Baskervilles*. In a later story it was revealed that Holmes had survived the plunge into the Reichenbach Falls.

Over the decades, it has become clear that the great detective will never die again—at least not in the minds and hearts of his readers. Sir Arthur Conan Doyle spent the last ten years of his life writing and lecturing about spiritualism, the belief that spirits of the dead can communicate with the living. He died on July 7, 1930. As for Holmes, the future held permanent retirement in Sussex, keeping bees.

The legend of Sherlock Holmes has lived on in movies, plays, television and radio shows, and other adaptations of his sleuthing adventures. There has been a Broadway musical and even a ballet. The 60 original stories have never been out of print, and a

Holmes studies an important clue in *A Study in Scarlet*—the master detective's first adventure. What does "Rache" mean? Elementary! It's German for "revenge."

number of biographies—both of Conan Doyle and of Holmes himself—have been written. And then there are hundreds of literary societies and other special groups throughout the world devoted to Sherlock Holmes. The most famous is called the Baker Street Irregulars, named after the street urchins who gathered information for the great detective.

The 100th anniversary of *A Study in Scarlet* was marked by countless special events and commemorations. Meanwhile, as ever, the mail continued to pour into 221B Baker Street.

JEFFREY H. HACKER
Author, *Carl Sandburg*

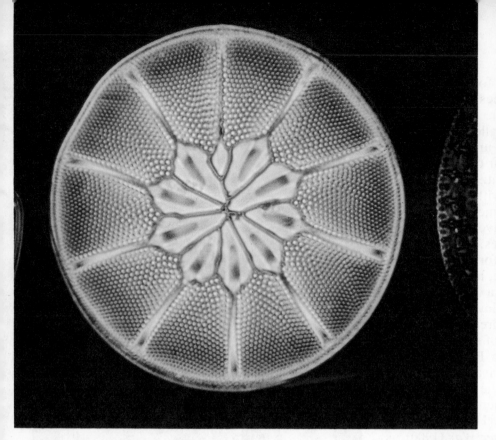

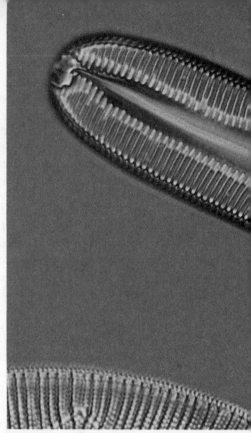

DIATOMS—
GLASSY BEAUTIES

If you've ever looked along the shore of a pond or beneath an ocean pier, you may have seen brown slime coating the rocks and pilings. Did you know that the slime was made up of beautiful living things like those pictured here?

These are diatoms, microscopic one-celled plants that live by the billions in water and damp places. Some are free-floating, and some hang together in chains. Diatoms are at the heart of the ocean food chain—they're eaten by small sea animals, which are in turn eaten by larger fish.

Diatoms are unusual plants. Their most intriguing features are their cell walls, or shells. Diatoms are plants in glass houses—their cell walls are made of silica, the same material used in glass. The shell comes in two halves that fit together like the top and bottom of a pillbox. There are more than 10,000 kinds of diatoms, but each one has a uniquely constructed shell. Because diatom shells are nearly colorless, photographers use colored lights and other tricks to capture their glassy beauty.

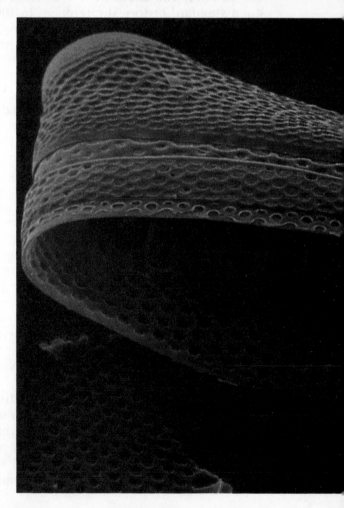

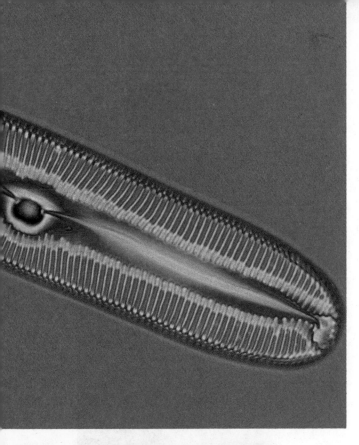

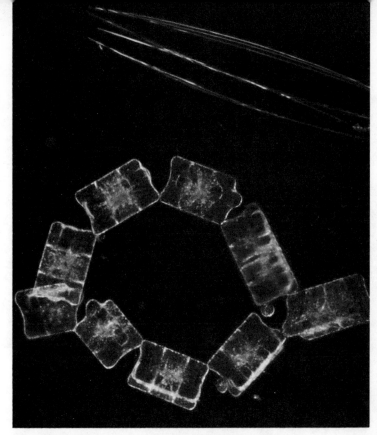

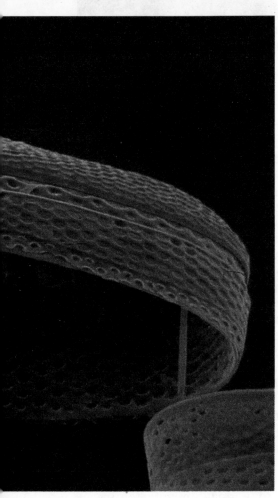

Animal noses do more than just sniff. When friendly elephants meet, for example, they twist their trunks together in an affectionate greeting—one of the many uses of an elephant's talented nose.

WHO NOSE?

Animal noses come in hundreds of different sizes and shapes, from a pig's stubby snout to an elephant's huge trunk. But animal noses aren't just for sniffing. They're designed to perform a wide variety of jobs.

Noses serve as hands, arms, tools, and weapons. They're used to dig, probe, spear, cut, tear, drill, crack, spray, strain, snorkel, and net. Some animals fight with their noses. Some rely on their noses to greet friends, warn enemies, spank youngsters, capture prey, or find their way home in the dark.

SUPER SNIFFERS. The human nose can distinguish thousands of different odors. That's good, but lots of animals can do better. Mammals like dogs, cats, pigs, and rats are much more sensitive to odors than we are. Smells guide these animals to their mates, warn them of their enemies, and help them find food.

A dog's cool, moist nose may not seem large, but it's crammed with smell-sensitive tissue. Inside the nose, this tissue is arranged in many wrinkles and folds. Stretched out flat, it would be 40 times the size of the smell-sensitive tissue in a human nose.

A dog can sense odors that escape us. And it can analyze a complex mixture of many odors and concentrate on one of them. Sniffing through the woods, a hunting dog will pick up the scent of a rabbit that may have hopped by an hour earlier. The dog can tell which way the rabbit was going, then follow the scent.

The champion sniffers among dogs are St. Bernards and bloodhounds. A St. Bernard can smell the victim of an avalanche under 20 feet (6 meters) of snow. A bloodhound can pick up the scent of a person from half a mile away. It can find a missing person by sniffing an article of clothing and then following the scent. Its sad-looking face helps its nose to do a good job—the bloodhound's droopy ears stir up scents from the ground, and its wrinkled skin traps those scents.

Compared to a dog, an anteater has a

highly specialized nose: Its nose is meant to sniff out termites and ants. In South America, the giant anteater shuffles along with its long snout close to the ground. When it sniffs an ant or termite mound, it scratches and digs with its claws, tearing away huge chunks of earth. Then the anteater's long sticky tongue flicks into the inside of the mound and laps up hundreds of insects and their eggs.

Another extra-long nose belongs to the little elephant shrew, which has a trunk like an elephant and long hind legs like a kangaroo, but is no bigger than a rat. The elephant shrew twitches and turns its trunklike nose as it sniffs for insects on the forest floor.

Like many mammals, fish also have a powerful sense of smell. Since they breathe with their gills, they use the nostrils on their snouts strictly for smelling.

A shark has one of the keenest noses of any animal. It can sniff one ounce of fish blood in a million ounces of sea water. It can pick up this scent from more than a quarter-mile away. And once it smells blood, it swims to the source like a guided missile.

Salmon use their noses as amazingly accurate direction finders. When they return from their ocean migrations, they locate their home stream from among hundreds of others by nosing in on its special smell.

ELEPHANTS' TRUNKS. No nose is more useful than an elephant's talented trunk. And no nose is bigger. The trunk of a full-grown elephant can be up to six feet (2 meters) long!

Since it's shaped like a rubber hose, a trunk can bend in almost any direction. When testing for smells, the trunk weaves through the air like a cobra and bends toward the source of every interesting odor. An elephant can check for the smell of food, water, friends, or enemies without even moving its head.

The nostrils at the tip of the trunk can pick up the scent of water 3 miles (5 kilometers) away. They can sniff a person several miles downwind. By smelling a bush or tree, an elephant can tell instantly if the leaves or fruit are good to eat.

Along with its two nostrils, an elephant also has one or two small fleshy "fingers" at the tip of its trunk. The African elephant has two of these fingerlike projections, the Indian elephant only one. With them, an elephant can reach down to pull grass, or reach up to pluck leaves or fruit. The "fingers" are so sensitive and their touch is so delicate that they can pick up an object as dainty as a peanut and carry it to the elephant's mouth.

While the tip of the trunk is sensitive, the trunk itself has plenty of muscle power. Reaching high into a tree, an elephant can

An anteater has a highly specialized nose—it sniffs out termites and ants from the ground.

The little elephant shrew has kangaroo legs and an elephant nose. Its trunklike snout is a good insect-sniffer.

rip off a big leafy branch and bring it down to earth. Its trunk has more than 40,000 muscles and is powerful enough to lift a ton of logs.

When an elephant visits a water hole, it draws the water into its trunk, which holds about a gallon and a half. Then it puts the trunk deep into its mouth and squirts the water down its throat. It takes 20 or 30 squirts to satisfy an elephant-sized thirst.

On hot days, elephants use their trunks to spray cooling water across their ears and backs. They're good swimmers, and in deep water they may hold their trunks above the surface and use them as snorkels. After a swim, an elephant likes to roll in the mud and finish its grooming session with a nice dust bath. It sucks up sand or dirt with its trunk and blows it over its body to help keep biting insects away.

An elephant also "talks" through its trunk, using it to scream with rage or squeal with pleasure. Male elephants, or bulls, test each other's strength by locking trunks in a giant-sized tug-of-war. Mother elephants ca-ress their babies with a soft touch of their trunks. They punish them with a swift, hard whack. When a herd is on the move, the baby follows along by gripping its mother's tail with its trunk. And when friendly elephants meet, they twist their trunks together in an affectionate elephant greeting.

It takes several months for a baby elephant to learn how to use its trunk properly. Since a full-sized trunk is a fairly heavy burden, an elephant may carry its trunk by resting it across its tusks.

As you might suspect, a sleeping elephant snores loudly through its trunk. And when an elephant sneezes, watch out!

BEAKS AND BILLS. A bird's nose is where its mouth is. Its beak or bill is actually a combination of nostrils and lips. Beaks are made of hardened epidermis, or skin, attached to the bird's jaws.

The beak is important to a bird because it serves as both a hand and a tool. Birds use their beaks to find, catch, kill, and eat their food. Simply by looking at a beak, you can often tell what kind of food the bird likes to eat.

Among birds of prey, the beak is a sharp-edged meat hook. An owl or hawk uses its hooked beak to tear a freshly killed mouse or rabbit into convenient bite-sized pieces.

Seed-eating birds like sparrows or cardinals have short, fat, nutcracker beaks that are strong enough to crush a cherry pit. And a woodpecker has a pointed chisel of a beak that's made for drilling holes in tree trunks. The woodpecker then laps up grubs and insects with a long, barbed, sticky tongue.

Some beaks are designed for probing, poking, or pulling. A curlew uses its long curved beak to pull crabs out of deep mud and crickets out of tall grass. A hummingbird pokes its slim beak into flowers, then flicks out its long tongue and sips up the sweet nectar. And an oystercatcher jabs its pointed beak into partly open oyster shells, paralyzing the oyster before it can snap shut.

The spoonbill's beak resembles a long serving spoon. When feeding, the bird moves its slightly open beak from side to side in wide arcs, sifting the shallow waters for small fish, insects, and other food. The spoonbill also uses its beak to make loud clapping noises when it returns to the nest and greets its mate.

A spoonbill's beak resembles a long serving spoon, and it's used to sift for food in shallow waters.

The drooping nose of a proboscis monkey may grow so long that the animal must push it aside in order to eat.

The long hooked beak of a pelican, with its big flabby pouch, makes an excellent fishing net. White pelicans often fish in groups. They form a semicircle offshore and beat the water with their wings, driving fish into the shallows, then scooping them up with a dip-net motion of their gaping pouches.

Before swallowing a fish, a pelican raises its beak to drain water out of the pouch. That's the moment when a bold seagull may swoop down to snatch the fish from the pelican's pouch.

It's true that a pelican's beak holds more than its "bellican"—a white pelican has a pouch capacity of three gallons, and a stomach capacity of only half that much.

The spectacular, brightly colored beak of the South American toucan is useful too. Notice the saw-tooth edges of the beak. They're designed to slice and dice fruits, insects, lizards, and small snakes in the woodlands where the toucan lives.

With a giant beak like that, a toucan can reach for fruit that might be hard to get otherwise. This bird will often pick a small fruit, toss it into the air, then catch it with its open beak. Toucans also like to duel with their beaks. Two rival birds will knock beaks together like a couple of practiced swordsmen.

In some toucans, the beak is as long and bulky as the rest of the body, giving the bird a rather top-heavy appearance. Luckily, the beak is honeycombed with air pockets and is almost as light as foam rubber. If it were much heavier, the big-beaked toucan would fall on its nose.

NOSES THAT SOUND OFF. A proboscis monkey is born with a cute turned-up nose. But as the monkey grows up, its nose grows down-ward. By the time a monkey is fully grown, its nose may hang down over its mouth. It may be so long that the monkey has to push it aside to eat. That's why these animals are called proboscis monkeys. "Proboscis" means "long snout."

These monkeys live along rivers and swamps on the island of Borneo in Southeast Asia. And they use their drooping noses to magnify their calls and cries. When a male

The "horns" jutting up from the tip of a rhinoceros viper's snout help to camouflage the reptile in its environment.

honks to call his mate or to warn a rival away from his territory, his long nose fills with sound and acts as an echo chamber. The nose makes the sound of the call louder.

The male elephant seal also has a noisy proboscis. During the mating season, he uses his trunklike nose to make long trumpeting sounds, warning rival males to stay away.

Bats use their noses in a form of sonar. As they fly through the night, they blow great bursts of supersonic sound through their nostrils. The sounds bounce back from any object in the bat's path, and its sensitive ears pick up the echoes.

These echoes keep the bat from flying into obstacles and help it find food. With its nose as a navigational guide, a bat can fly through a dense forest in total darkness without touching a tree. Listening to echoes, it can nose in on a flying insect up to 15 feet (4.5 meters) away.

NOSES TO HIDE BEHIND. The spatulate-nosed tree frog has a nose shaped like a flat spoon, or spatula. When the weather is hot and dry, the frog finds a hole in some rocks and crawls inside. Then it plugs up the entrance with its flat nose. Protected from the sun and wind, the frog can keep its body cool and moist.

The rhinoceros viper has "horns" that jut up from the tip of its snout. This 4-foot (1-meter) long poisonous African snake lives among thorny, spiky plants. As it lies in ambush, waiting to strike out at passing prey, its horny snout helps it blend into the background.

DANGEROUS NOSES. The African three-horned chameleon uses its nose as a weapon. It has a pointed horn at the tip of its snout, with two other horns just above it. It can mount a three-pronged attack when it defends its territory from rivals, charging headlong with its nose.

Among certain kinds of tropical termites, the soldier termites have heads shaped like squirt guns, with snouts like nozzles. When ants or other enemies invade the termites' nest, these soldiers rush forward and squirt a sticky substance from their snouts, trapping the ants or driving them away.

A BORING NOSE. The female snout beetle, or acorn weevil, uses her long tubelike snout to prepare a home for the next generation. With her snout, she bores a hole into an acorn.

With 22 fleshy feelers circling its nostrils, the star-nosed mole wins the prize for the strangest-looking nose!

Then she turns around and drops an egg down the hole. When the egg hatches, the young larva lives safely inside the acorn shell until it has eaten up all the meat.

A STAR AMONG NOSES. The prize for the strangest-looking nose of all goes to the star-nosed mole. This animal has 22 fleshy feelers forming a ring around its nostrils. The two top feelers are held rigidly forward. The rest wiggle constantly as the mole searches for worms and insects to eat.

Moles live in dark underground burrows. The star-nosed mole is nearly blind. It finds its way and its food with the twitching feelers that fringe its nostrils.

While its nose may look odd, it really works. A star-nosed mole finds and eats half its weight in insects and grubs every day.

RUSSELL FREEDMAN
Author, *Animal Superstars*

E FOR EXCELLENCE

Surnames beginning with the letter E aren't as plentiful as those beginning with many other letters of the alphabet. Nevertheless, a quick look through an encyclopedia or a biographical dictionary shows that many outstanding people have E surnames. Amelia Earhart, the famous aviator, is an example. So are the 22 other people listed below (in the left column). Match each person to his or her accomplishment (in the right column).

1. Eakins, Thomas
2. Eames, Charles
3. Earhart, Amelia
4. Eastman, George
5. Eastwood, Clint
6. Edison, Thomas Alva
7. Eiffel, Alexandre
8. Einstein, Albert
9. Eisenhower, Dwight D.
10. Eliot, T. S.
11. Ellington, Duke
12. Ellison, Ralph
13. Emerson, Ralph Waldo
14. Erasmus, Desiderius
15. Ericson, Leif
16. Ernst, Max
17. Ervin, Sam
18. Erving, Julius
19. Euclid
20. Euripides
21. Evans, Mary Ann
22. Evers, Medgar
23. Evert, Chris

a. Invented the first simple, reliable camera
b. Civil rights leader
c. French engineer
d. Basketball player nicknamed Doctor J
e. Dutch scholar during the Renaissance
f. Furniture designer
g. 34th president of the United States
h. Tennis player
i. Movie star and mayor of Carmel, California
j. Surrealist painter and sculptor
k. Dramatist of ancient Greece
l. Mathematician of ancient Greece
m. First woman pilot to cross the Atlantic
n. Scientist known for theory of relativity
o. Viking explorer of North America
p. Author of *The Waste Land*
q. Novelist better known as George Eliot
r. American realist artist of the 1800's
s. Author of *Invisible Man*
t. Invented the first phonograph
u. Jazz musician and composer
v. U.S. Senator who headed Watergate investigation
w. Wrote the poem "The Concord Hymn"

ANSWERS: 1,r; 2,f; 3,m; 4,a; 5,i; 6,t; 7,c; 8,n; 9,g; 10,p; 11,u; 12,s; 13,w; 14,e; 15,o; 16,j; 17,v; 18,d; 19,l; 20,k; 21,q; 22,b; 23,h.

Next, go on a hunt. The last names of all 23 people are hidden in this search-a-word puzzle. Try to find them. Cover the puzzle with a sheet of tracing paper. Read forward, backward, up, down, and diagonally. Then draw a neat line through each name as you find it. One name has been shaded in for you.

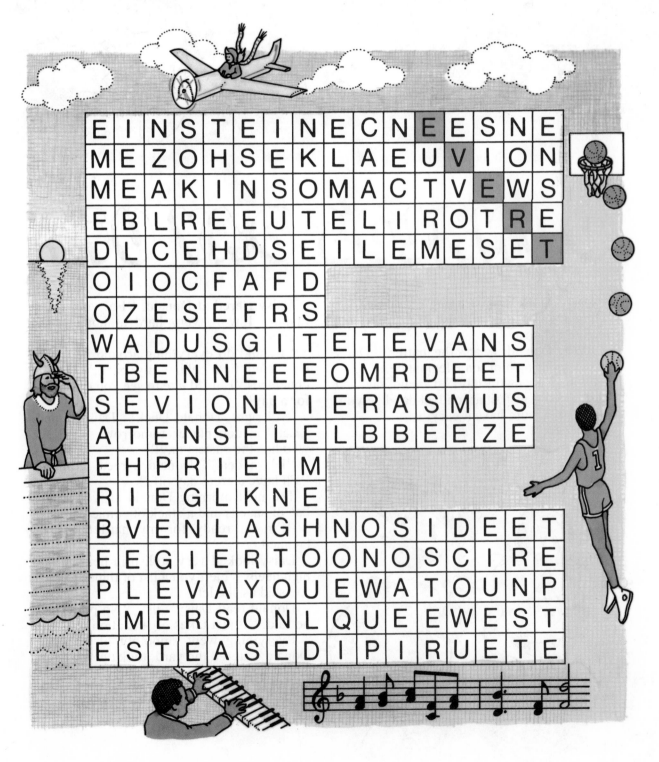

DONALD'S DAY OFF

Daisy Duck was relaxing one afternoon when Donald dropped by after work. He looked exhausted.

"Why Donald, what's the matter?" Daisy asked, pouring him some lemonade.

"I had an awful day," Donald said. "I wish I could just sit around all day like you, Daisy. You sure have it easy."

Daisy glared at Donald. "For your information, I work very hard at home," she snapped.

"I could do everything around here with one hand tied behind my back," Donald chuckled. "But I'd like to see you do my job for a day!"

"All right, Donald Duck!" Daisy fumed. "Let's switch places tomorrow. We'll see who has the easiest day!"

"It's a deal," Donald agreed, grinning. "I'll have a great day off."

The next morning Donald arrived with a bag of snacks and a stack of comic books.

"I'm all ready for my hard day," he laughed.

Daisy looked very stylish in her suit and high heels. "I left you a list of things to do," she said as she left.

Donald read Daisy's list. "No problem," he said. "It just takes organization."

Everything went smoothly for a while. Donald watered the yard, took out the trash, and washed the breakfast dishes.

Then he decided to take a break. He made a snack and lay down to read his comic books.

Before he knew it, Donald fell asleep. When he woke, it was late.

But Donald still wasn't worried. He checked Daisy's list. All that was left for him to do was to wash the laundry and vacuum the living room.

"This is so easy," he thought. "I'll show Daisy. I'll cook dinner, too."

As Donald read Daisy's cookbooks, he heard her cat and dog at the kitchen door. They were hungry.

Donald looked at the list. "Oops, I forgot to feed the cat and dog," he said. "Sorry, fellows."

"The cat and dog get in the way in the kitchen," Daisy had written. "Be sure to feed them outside."

"Oh, they won't bother me," Donald thought. He let the animals into the kitchen. He fed them and returned to his cooking.

"First I'll fix the fanciest dessert Daisy has ever eaten!" he decided. "Chocolate whipped cream marshmallow soufflé à la Donald!"

Donald got eggs, milk, and whipped cream from the refrigerator. He got a bowl, sugar, and flour from the pantry. He mixed and stirred and mixed some more.

"I'll double everything in the recipe, and make a super soufflé," he said. "Daisy will be twice as impressed!"

He broke more eggs, poured more milk, and measured more sugar.

The animals watched Donald stir and mix.

The cat rubbed against Donald's legs, meowing for a taste. The dog wagged his tail and begged.

"Go away," Donald fussed at them. They didn't move.

Just then the doorbell rang. Donald left the bowl of batter on the kitchen table and went to answer it.

A delivery boy was at the door with a package. Donald carried the package into the living room.

"While I'm here, I might as well start the laundry and do the vacuuming," Donald decided, forgetting all about the soufflé.

In the laundry room, he found a big pile of sheets, towels, and clothing.

"It'll take me too long to do all this laundry separately," he thought. "I'll wash it all at once to save time."

Donald stuffed everything into the washing machine until it was so full he couldn't close the lid. He read the directions on the soap box. "Use one cup of soap for each load of clothes," it said.

"Let's see, I have four loads of clothes," Donald figured. "If I use four times as much soap, everything will come out clean!"

Donald poured in lots and lots of soap and started the machine. It made loud, groaning noises, but Donald paid no attention.

The vacuuming was next.

"Please do a very good job on my brand new braided rug," Daisy had written.

Donald plugged in the vacuum cleaner. It was very big, very heavy, and very hard to push. By the time Donald got to Daisy's rug, he was tired.

"Whew, vacuuming is hard work!" he thought.

As he rested, he remembered the soufflé.

"Goodness!" Donald exclaimed. "I have to put that soufflé in the oven now, or it'll never be done in time!" He left the vacuum running and ran to the kitchen.

But the soufflé was gone! And the cat and dog were happily licking their whiskers.

Donald was furious. He chased the animals outside and started the soufflé all over again, working as fast as he could.

Donald looked at the recipe. "Bake the soufflé at 350 degrees for one hour," it said. Donald looked at the clock. It was almost time for Daisy to come home!

"I'll have to turn the heat up twice as high for the soufflé to be done on time," Donald thought. He popped it into the oven and turned the heat as high as it would go.

Just then he heard a loud clunking and chugging sound in the living room. He dashed in just in time to see Daisy's new rug disappearing into the vacuum. The machine was rumbling as if it would explode any second.

"Wak!" Donald squawked. He grabbed the last inch of the rug just before it disappeared. Donald pulled and tugged with all his might!

"Pwofp!" The rug came loose so fast that Donald sat down hard on the floor.

Then he realized that his tailfeathers were wet! To his horror, soapy water was running across the floor.

82

"Oh, no!" Donald scrambled to his feet and sloshed to the laundry room. Water was pouring from the machine. Splashing and squawking, Donald began mopping as fast as he could.

As he mopped, Donald smelled something funny. He dropped the mop and raced to the kitchen.

"My soufflé is burning!" Donald cried, throwing open the door. Black smoke billowed from the oven.

Coughing and gasping, Donald grabbed the pan full of gooey, burnt soufflé and tossed it in the sink.

Just then, Daisy drove up!

"I had a wonderful day," she called, as she came in. Then she gasped!

"What have you done to my house!" Daisy cried.

Black smoke filled the house. Soapy wet footprints ran across the floor. Her new rug was tangled in a corner. And Donald was sitting in the middle of the mess with a dazed expression.

"I'm sorry, Daisy," he gulped. "I guess I'd better go now."

Daisy looked at Donald. He was such a mess, she had to smile. But she wanted to teach him a lesson.

"Wait a minute," she said. "You've been relaxing here all day while I worked. I'm hungry. What's for dinner?"

Sheepishly, Donald pointed to the soufflé in the sink.

"We can't eat that," she said. "We'd better go out for a pizza."

Donald's face brightened. He grabbed his hat. "Gee, thanks," he said. "I love pizza!"

"Good," Daisy said. "Because you're treating!" She started to giggle.

"Okay," Donald began to laugh too. "I'll even buy dessert!"

A SALUTE TO THE CONSTITUTION

Through the summer of 1787, a group of men met in Philadelphia's Independence Hall. Their goal was to hammer out a new form of government for the fledgling United States, which had won its independence from Britain just six years before. The job wasn't an easy one—the heat of the delegates' debates was matched only by the sweltering summer weather outside the high-ceilinged room where they gathered. But in the end, they succeeded.

They produced a document that established the framework of the country, truly joining the states together into a nation for the first time. The document—four sheets of parchment, hand-written with a feather quill—was the Constitution of the United States. At the time, the Constitution was something of an experiment. It was filled with compromises, and few of the delegates agreed with all its provisions. George Washington himself said that he didn't expect it to last more than twenty years. But the Constitution survived, and it shaped the nation.

In 1987, people in the United States celebrated the Constitution's 200th anniversary with ceremonies, events, and renewed interest in the document itself. Philadelphia, naturally, was the site of some of the most important events. The city staged exhibits, parades, concerts, various shows and re-enactments, and even a mock constitutional convention for high school students. Other communities and states also planned events.

One goal of the bicentennial events was to increase public knowledge of the Constitution. Polls showed that many people were ignorant of some of its basic provisions. (Only four of every ten people polled, for example, knew that the first ten amendments make up the Bill of Rights.) So as part of the celebration, millions of copies of the document were distributed. And there was fresh interest in what some people have called a miracle—the story of how the group of men in Philadelphia overcame their differences to draw up the Constitution.

A NATION IN TROUBLE

The Constitutional Convention was called because the United States was in trouble. Since independence, the thirteen original states had been governed under the Articles of Confederation. Under this constitution, each state was practically a separate power, bound into a loose association with the others. The U.S. government consisted of a weak Congress that had very little power.

As a result, the states had begun to squabble among themselves. They argued over territory and levied taxes on trade that crossed state lines. Each state also issued its own currency, and some were printing quantities of paper money that quickly became worthless. Congress had no power to stop these acts. Moreover, Congress couldn't levy direct taxes—it could only ask for assessments from the states, based on the states' own estimates of what they could afford to pay. The new government was therefore practically broke—it even owed money to soldiers who had fought in the Revolutionary War.

In 1786, a brief but violent uprising of farmers in Massachusetts (Shays' Rebellion) created grave new worries about the country's future. There were also threats along the borders: Spain had closed the lower Mississippi River to American ships, choking off trade. Britain, violating an agreement made at the end of the Revolutionary War, was refusing to give up forts in the Northwest Territory, thus blocking American expansion to the west.

If the United States was to survive and thrive, it seemed clear that a stronger central government would be needed. Some people even suggested a monarchy. But those who had fought to win freedom from Britain weren't ready to give up their democratic ideals. Instead, Congress called for a convention to amend and strengthen the Articles of Confederation.

THE CONVENTION

The 55 delegates who assembled in Philadelphia in the summer of 1787 represented twelve of the thirteen states. (Rhode Island refused to attend.) They included some of the most important and influential people in the country—lawyers, judges, landowners. Nearly all had held public office at some time. Washington came, although he was reluctant to leave his farm. Also on hand was Benjamin Franklin, 81 and so troubled by gout that he had to be carried about the city in a sedan chair. But most of the other delegates were relatively young—shy, soft-spoken James Madison, for example, was 36; the brilliant Alexander Hamilton, 32. A few major figures were missing. Thomas Jefferson was in Paris, as minister to France. And Patrick Henry refused to attend, saying that he "smelt a rat."

On May 25—a gray and rainy Friday—the convention opened. Washington was named presiding officer, and a few ground rules were adopted. One was that no vote would be final until the convention had a completed document before it; until then, the delegates could change their minds on any provision.

Another rule was that the proceedings would take place in absolute secrecy. Jefferson wrote from Paris that he was "sorry they began their deliberations by so abominable a precedent as that of tying up the tongues of their members." But Madison and other delegates believed that secrecy would allow the delegates to speak their minds freely at the convention. He later wrote that "no Constitution would ever have been adopted by the convention if the debates had been made public." His notes on the proceedings, which were published after his death, provide a detailed account of the convention.

In fact, Madison's ideas set the tone for the debates. His Virginia Plan, presented at the outset, called for a "national government, with a supreme legislative, executive and judiciary." That idea went much farther than amending the Articles of Confederation—it was a call to throw the old constitution out the window and begin all over again.

Most of the delegates agreed that strong measures were necessary. But what form should the new government take? Madison's plan called for a strong bicameral (two-house) legislature and a weaker executive. Representatives in the legislature would be elected by proportional representation—that is, more seats for the more populous states. But delegates from the small states objected strongly. William Paterson of New Jersey, for example, said he would never consent to the plan because his state "would be swallowed up."

There was also debate on how the representatives should be elected. Some delegates viewed the "people" as uneducated, and they were against direct elections (by popular vote). "The evils we experience flow from the excess of democracy," said Elbridge Gerry of Massachusetts. But others believed that the support of the people was essential for the new government.

The convention nearly foundered on these issues. But in the end, the delegates agreed on a compromise that was proposed by Roger Sherman of Connecticut. It called for a House of Representatives with proportional representation, elected by popular vote, and a Senate in which all states would have equal representation. Senators were to be chosen by the state legislatures (the system was later changed to direct elections).

The legislature wasn't the only issue that provoked argument. It took the delegates 60 votes to decide how the President should be picked, how much power he should have, how long his term should be, and whether he could be impeached. Everyone knew that Washington, the most respected and best-known person in the country, would most likely be the first President. But, as Benjamin Franklin put it, "The first man put at the helm will be a good one. Nobody knows what sort may come afterwards."

200 YEARS AGO . . .

While the framers of the Constitution debated, daily life went on outside Independence Hall. Here are some items that were in use in 1787: Instead of a purse, a woman used a lady's pocket. It tied around the waist and was worn under her dress . . . This baby's bottle is made of pewter. Most families had seven to ten babies, but many didn't live to adulthood . . . Ice skates like this one, with its elegant curled toe, tied on with leather straps and required strong ankles . . . Chamber pots took the place of indoor plumbing and came in all shapes, even a porcelain cat. Corn husks and newsprint were used as toilet paper.

The convention also divided sharply on the subject of slavery. Some delegates wanted the Constitution to outlaw slavery; others wanted a clause that would sanction it. Again, a compromise was reached: Congress would be forbidden from outlawing slavery until 1808.

Not all the delegates stayed through the long debates. Many came and went as personal business allowed. Some, including Alexander Hamilton, despaired of ever seeing the convention finish its work and left altogether. (Hamilton later returned.) Those who stayed in Philadelphia generally met six days a week. They struggled with constitu-

tional questions—and the heat—from 10 A.M. to 3 or 4 P.M., when they adjourned for hearty dinners at the City Tavern, the Black Horse, the George, and other popular inns.

When the delegates had finally reached agreement on the Constitution's provisions, the final wording was entrusted to Gouverneur Morris of Pennsylvania. He wrote the famous preamble that begins "We the People . . ." And on September 12, 1787, the finished Constitution was presented to the delegates.

Even then, there were disagreements. Some felt the document was too vague. George Mason of Virginia called for a bill of rights. Madison wanted provisions for a national university. But most of the delegates wanted to finish and go home. On September 17, all but three signed the document. Franklin summed up the feelings of many when he told Washington, "I consent, sir, to this Constitution because I expect no better."

A FLEXIBLE CONSTITUTION

The new Constitution still faced major hurdles: approval by Congress and nine of the thirteen states. The public debates it produced were, if possible, even more heated than the secret discussions of the convention. But by June 21, 1788, the Constitution had been ratified (approved) by the required nine. Two key states, Virginia and New York, gave their approval soon after.

Within two years, the Constitution was widely accepted and respected. It had also begun to change—the first ten amendments, making up the Bill of Rights, were adopted in 1789. Over the following years, sixteen other amendments were adopted. They outlawed slavery, gave women the right to vote, lowered the voting age to 18, and made other alterations. The government created by the Constitution changed in some ways, too. For example, both the executive and judicial branches gradually grew stronger than was originally envisioned.

But the basic provisions of the Constitution remained, and they proved flexible enough to serve as the supreme law of the land for 200 years. Today there are many calls for changes, even for a second constitutional convention. Some people want to add specific provisions, such as an amendment requiring a balanced federal budget. Others feel the system of government needs changing. They argue that the three-branch system, set up to provide checks and balances in power, now produces stalemates—so that nothing gets done.

But the calls for change worry other people, who fear that too much tinkering with the Constitution may destroy the democratic system of government that has worked well in the United States. The Constitution, they argue, is a delicate instrument. The fact that it has survived so long and worked so well is proof that the delegates of 1787 were far more successful than they ever could have imagined.

Red, white, and blue balloons form a giant flag in front of Independence Hall, in celebration of the bicentennial.

We the People

INTERPRETING THE CONSTITUTION

The U.S. Constitution provides a general plan of government. Many of its clauses are broadly phrased, and they can be interpreted in more than one way. Moreover, the Constitution today must be adapted to developments—from television news to computer record-keeping—that could never have been foreseen in 1787. Thus disputes often arise over what the Constitution truly means.

The final say in such matters belongs to the U.S. Supreme Court. The Constitution established the Supreme Court as "the judicial power of the United States." But the Court's role in interpreting the Constitution wasn't fully spelled out in the document. Thus, "Equal Justice Under Law"—the saying engraved on the Supreme Court building in Washington, D.C.—hasn't always been an easy principle to apply.

The Supreme Court's role was more firmly established in the first years after the Constitution was adopted. In the famous case *Marbury* versus *Madison* (1803), the first chief justice, John Marshall, ruled that the Court has the power to decide if an existing law violates the Constitution. Using this power, called judicial review, the Court has since overturned more than 100 acts of Congress, as well as executive actions and many state laws.

The Court is made up of nine justices (one chief and eight associates), who are chosen by the President with the approval of the Senate. They make constitutional rulings only when actual cases are presented to them. Most cases are appeals to overturn rulings that were made by lower courts. Usually, the Court selects just 150 to 180 of the 5,000 cases submitted each year.

In each of the cases, the justices hear the arguments on both sides of the dispute. They study the records of the case, the Constitution, and any relevant laws and precedents (similar cases that have been previously decided). Then they meet to discuss the case. When the outcome has been decided, one of the justices writes the majority opinion. (Justices who disagree with the ruling, or agree with it on other grounds, may write separate opinions.)

Supreme Court rulings on constitutional matters are final—short of amending the Constitution itself, there is no way to overturn them. But occasionally the Court overrules itself. For example, in 1896, in *Plessy* versus *Ferguson,* the Court ruled that segregation between blacks and whites didn't violate the Constitution. In 1954, in *Brown* versus *Board of Education of Topeka,* it found that segregation was unconstitutional.

The example shows that Supreme Court interpretations change with the times. And because justices are appointed by whatever President is in power when an opening comes up, the interpretations may also change with the political mood of the country. But because an appointment to the Court is an appointment for life, openings are few, and change is slow.

Some observers feel that in recent years the Court has moved from broad, liberal interpretations to narrower, more conservative rulings. This trend was much in the news in 1987, when Associate Justice Lewis F. Powell, Jr., resigned. President Ronald Reagan nominated Robert H. Bork, a judge and legal scholar known for his strong conservative views, to take his place. The Senate, however, didn't confirm the appointment, because a number of senators feared his vote would tip the balance of the Court and cause it to overturn many of its past rulings.

Whether conservative or liberal, however, Supreme Court rulings must in the end be based on the Constitution. Following are two famous Supreme Court cases. Before you read how the Court ruled in each case, take a few minutes to decide

Equal Justice Under Law

how you would rule. If you're in doubt, refer to the Constitution—especially the Bill of Rights—for help in deciding.

IN RE GAULT (1967)

This case involves issues of the Fifth, Sixth, and Fourteenth amendments, which protect the rights of people accused of crimes.

The Facts. Gerald Gault, 15, was arrested for making obscene phone calls and was brought before a judge in an Arizona juvenile court. He wasn't given a chance to have a lawyer, and the judge didn't explain exactly what he was charged with. His accuser (who had received the phone calls) didn't appear in court to say what he had done wrong. But Gault had previously been arrested for purse-snatching. Based on his two arrests, a police officer told the court that he was a delinquent. He was sentenced to a state reform school, where he could be held until age 21.

A retired lawyer stepped in and appealed the decision on Gault's behalf. It eventually reached the Supreme Court.

The Arguments. Gault's lawyer argued that he had been denied "due process"—that is, his case hadn't been decided in the legal way. Under the Sixth Amendment, a person accused of a crime is entitled to have a lawyer, to hear the charges against him, and to confront his or her accusers.

Lawyers for the State of Arizona argued that juvenile courts are different from adult courts. To help young people straighten out, they said, judges must be free to decide what is best, in much the same way that parents decide what is best for their children.

How would you decide?

The Ruling. The Supreme Court ruled 7–2 in Gault's favor. It said that juveniles, just like adults, have a right to have lawyers, hear the charges against them, and question their accusers. This case became a landmark in juvenile justice.

NEW YORK TIMES V. UNITED STATES (1971)

This case, known as the Pentagon Papers case, concerns issues of the First Amendment, which protects freedom of speech, press, and religion.

The Facts. In 1971, *The New York Times* obtained a copy of a secret government study that detailed the development of U.S. policy in Vietnam. (The report, known as the Pentagon Papers, covered the years 1945–68.) When the newspaper began to run a series of articles based on the study, the federal government went to a district court and got a temporary order blocking further publication. The court that imposed the order later lifted it, but an appeals court re-imposed it. The *Times* appealed to the Supreme Court. (A second newspaper, the *Washington Post,* had also run articles on the study and had run into similar problems. The Court heard both cases together.)

The Arguments. Lawyers for the newspapers argued that the ban on publication amounted to censorship—that is, the government was deciding what could and could not be printed. Government control of the press is forbidden by the First Amendment. If the ban stood, it would mark the first time that a court had ordered a newspaper not to print something.

Lawyers for the government argued that the United States would be damaged if the information in the report was made public. They said that publication would create a serious threat to national security and might even affect the lives of U.S. soldiers who were then fighting in Vietnam.

Who was right?

The Ruling. The Supreme Court ruled 6–3 in favor of the newspapers. It said that the government had failed to show good reason for overriding the First Amendment. Several justices wrote opinions saying that the publication of information couldn't be blocked unless it would do grave and immediate harm, such as costing lives. The government hadn't proved that such a danger existed.

SHOPPING BAG ART

Who doesn't have a shopping bag or two folded away in a drawer or on a closet shelf? After you carry your purchases home from the store, a shopping bag has dozens of uses —beach bag, tote bag, picnic carrier, storage container, and more. But you might want to take your bags out of the closet and give them a closer look: Shopping bags are also portable art.

From humble beginnings as brown paper satchels, shopping bags have evolved into colorful, eye-catching graphic presentations. Some mimic the styles of famous artists or reproduce their works. Some feature cartoon characters. Many bags, however, are original creations, making use of the latest trends in design.

Most shopping bags are made of heavy paper, but plastic, cloth, and metallic foil are also used. Some of the most eye-catching bags are put out by department stores, which use specially designed bags to advertise promotions and certain shopping seasons, such as Christmas. But all sorts of shops offer bags—and, generally, the more exclusive the shop, the more elaborate and unusual the bag. Museums, libraries, and even political groups have used shopping bags for promotions. And greeting card stores sell bags to use in place of gift wrap.

As shopping bags have become more fanciful, many people have come to appreciate them for their design qualities and even to collect them. Among the collectors of shopping bag art is the Smithsonian Institution, which recently staged a touring exhibit of hundreds of bags. So hang on to your shopping bags—you may have the start of an art collection in your closet.

PLANT PUZZLES

• How can a plant reproduce if its seeds never fall to the ground?

• What do you get if you cross a firefly with a tobacco plant?

• Can a plant talk, or at least send out messages?

• What plant produces the world's largest flower?

These questions may sound as if they come from a trivia game or a book of silly riddles. But in fact, scientific researchers have turned up fascinating—and surprising —answers to all these plant puzzles.

ROADBLOCKS TO REPRODUCTION

Flowering plants reproduce through pollination, usually with the help of insects. As insects fly from blossom to blossom to drink the sweet nectar produced by the flowers, they carry a few grains of pollen from the stamens of one bloom to the pistil (ovary) of the next. There, the pollen fertilizes eggs, which develop into seeds and fall to the ground. In time, the seeds grow into new plants.

This reproduction process is difficult for a beautiful South African shrub called *Gar-*

Only certain animals can help the lovely *Gardenia thunbergia* reproduce. This is because the flower's nectar is hard to reach in the long, thin tubes where it is produced; and the plant's seeds are contained in hard-shelled fruits that don't break open.

denia thunbergia. The first roadblock that the plant faces has to do with pollination. Unlike the flowers of cultivated gardenias, the flower of *thunbergia* is a long, thin tube topped by a ring of white petals. Nectar is produced at the base of the tube—well out of reach of most insects. But help comes from a long-tongued nocturnal moth. Some species of hawkmoths (sometimes called sphinx moths) have tongues up to 5½ inches (14 centimeters) long! It's easy for them to reach the nectar, and they carry pollen from shrub to shrub on their nighttime feeding rounds. (The moth's tongue, or proboscis, rolls into a neat coil when the insect isn't feeding.)

Gardenia thunbergia must get past yet another roadblock to reproduction. After the shrub has been pollinated, the seeds develop inside oval-shaped fruits, about 3 to 4 inches (7 to 10 centimeters) long. But the fruits have hard wooden shells that don't break open, and they never fall from the branches.

If the seeds never fall to the ground, how does the plant reproduce? Again, animals come to the rescue. The fruits are a favorite snack for several species of antelope and Cape buffalo. The animals chew open the woody shells and eat the seeds. Then, scientists think, the seeds pass through the animals' digestive tracts and are deposited on the ground. This unusual method of scattering seeds seems to be very successful—the *Gardenia thunbergia* is found throughout the high grasslands of southern and eastern Africa.

GROWING AND GLOWING

If you cross a firefly with a tobacco plant, you don't get a self-lighting cigarette. You get a tobacco plant that glows in the dark.

Scientists at the University of California at San Diego produced such plants in an experiment in genetic engineering. In genetic engineering, scientists alter genetic material or transplant genes from one cell to another. The field holds great potential in many areas, from farming to medicine.

The California scientists wanted to learn more about how genes work. All cells contain all the genes needed for all body functions. Cells perform different functions because only some of the genes are "switched on." Thus, in a plant, genes order

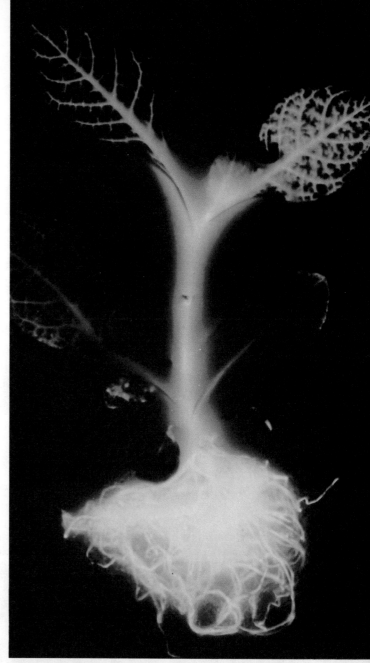

The light-producing gene from a cell of a firefly was transferred into the cells of a tobacco plant. The result: a tobacco plant that glows in the dark!

some cells to form leaves; others, stems; and still others, roots. But how—and when—are the genes that direct the cells turned on and off?

Most genes perform their jobs unseen, making it hard for scientists to study them. An exception is the gene that allows fireflies to produce light. Basically, the gene tells firefly cells to produce luciferase, an enzyme. When luciferase combines with oxygen and other chemicals in the cells, the firefly lights up.

The scientists reasoned that the luciferase gene was an ideal subject for genetic engineering because the light would make it easy to see whether the gene was working after a transplant. Using special chemicals, they "snipped" the gene from firefly cells and inserted it into the genetic material of a bacterium that infects plants. The bacterium containing the firefly gene was used to infect tobacco plant cells, which were then grown into full-fledged plants.

The last step in the experiment was to irrigate the plants with a solution containing the other chemicals found in a firefly's cells that are needed to produce the firefly's light. The result was a glowing tobacco plant. (The faint glow can be seen only in a dark room, and it is recorded with special photographic techniques.) The scientists now want to link the firefly gene to specific plant genes—such as those that order cells to form leaves. Thus they hope to be able to *see* how and when plant genes are turned on.

AN ALARM PLANT

Can a plant talk? Of course not. But a plant may be able to tell you something all the same. For example, researchers have found a plant that can sound an alarm—against air pollution.

The plant is *Tradescantia,* a hybrid form of the spiderwort, which is often found in the wild. *Tradescantia* looks quite ordinary: It has long, grassy leaves; waxy, knobby stems; and tiny bluish-lavender flowers. But in polluted air, the plant does something quite extraordinary—it changes color.

Tradescantia is a cross between a pink-flowering spiderwort and a blue-flowering spiderwort. The blue color is dominant, so in clean air the flowers are blue. But certain pollutants can alter the genes that determine flower color. If the plant is exposed to these pollutants just before it blooms, tiny hairs in the stamens (the pollen-bearing structures at the center of the flower) change from blue to pink.

The plant has great promise as a way of detecting harmful substances in the air. It's said to be sensitive to low-level radiation, pesticides, fungicides, and other harmful chemicals, as well as to ordinary industrial air pollution. And since no single plant species can be expected to react to all possible

The *tradescantia* is a hybrid form of the spiderwort, and its flowers are usually blue. But if the plant is exposed to certain pollutants before it blooms, the flowers turn pink.

Rafflesia arnoldii, a plant that grows in Indonesia, produces the largest flowers in the world. Not only are the flowers huge and exotic, they also have a distinctive smell—like rotten meat.

forms of pollution, scientists are testing other plants to see if they have similar talents. Among those being studied are corn, barley, and a variety of mustard plant. One day, it may be possible to monitor the quality of the air simply by looking at your garden.

THE WORLD'S LARGEST FLOWER

What plant produces the largest flower in the world? The answer to that trivia question is *Rafflesia arnoldii,* a plant that grows in the rain forests of Sumatra and Borneo, in Indonesia. But there's nothing trivial about the flowers—they can measure more than 3 feet (1 meter) across and weigh about 15 pounds (7 kilograms).

Rafflesia arnoldii was named for two British explorers, Sir Thomas Stamford Raffles and Dr. Joseph Arnold, who spotted it in southwestern Sumatra in 1818. Indonesians call it *bunga patma,* or lotus flower. It's quite rare. And as its rain-forest habitat is gradually destroyed by advancing civilization, it's becoming rarer still.

The plant is something of a mystery. It has no proper roots and no leaves to provide nourishment. Instead, it grows out of the roots or stems of certain tropical vines. Just how the tiny seeds take hold and start to grow is a bit of a puzzle in itself. But after about a year of growth inside the host plant, a bud about 2 inches (5 centimeters) wide bursts through the surface. The bud continues to grow for nine months before it opens completely to reveal its full splendor.

The flower is not only huge—it's exotic, with heavy reddish-brown petals marked by pale patches. It emits a distinctive scent that some people have compared to the odor of rotten meat. The scent has given rise to some other common names for the plant: corpse flower and stinking corpse lily. It also draws flies, which are the plant's chief pollinators. Some *Rafflesia* flowers are males and produce only pollen; others are females and produce only eggs. The flies must carry the pollen from one to the other.

Although it takes months to develop, the *Rafflesia* flower blooms for just four days and then dies. But if the plant is a female, it produces a fruit filled with thousands of seeds. The fruit ripens in about seven months, and the mysterious cycle of this exotic plant begins again.

SECRETS
OF SNOWFLAKES

If you've ever caught a snowflake on your mitten or your sleeve and stopped to look closely at it, you know how beautiful these delicate ice crystals are. Captured under a microscope, snowflakes reveal the full range of their beauty. Each is a crystal clear, intricate, six-pointed star, and each is different from the next.

Snowflakes are full of secrets. What causes them to form in six-sided shapes? What's responsible for their patterned beauty? Why do no two snowflakes look exactly the same? Scientists have puzzled over these questions for years. Now, with the help of computers and mathematical models, they've begun to find answers.

The birth of a snowflake begins after water evaporates from the surface of the earth and rises as much as 6 miles (10 kilometers) into the atmosphere. There, where temperatures are colder, the water vapor condenses into tiny droplets and forms clouds.

What happens next depends on the temperature. Below -40°F (-40°C), the droplets freeze instantly into ice crystals. At temperatures that are warmer but still below freezing, the droplets need a "seed"—a particle, such as a speck of dust—to freeze around. When a suitable particle comes along, the water droplets evaporate and recondense on the particle's surface. The specific structure and electrical charge of a water molecule cause all ice crystals to have a hexagonal (six-sided) shape.

Now the ice crystal begins to grow into a snowflake. Its final intricate design is determined by the changes in temperature and moisture the crystal encounters as it swirls around in the cloud and begins to fall to earth. As it descends, it picks up more water droplets. Most of the moisture condenses on the six corners of the hexagon because they stick out farthest. The corners begin to grow into long arms, or dendrites, each with a pattern of branches.

When the snowflake meets a change in temperature or moisture, its pattern of growth changes. No two snowflakes take exactly the same path to earth, so each encounters slightly different conditions. Thus each snowflake is slightly different from the next. But within each snowflake, all the dendrites encounter the same conditions at the same times, and they grow in almost exactly the same way. This is what makes the snowflake appear so symmetrical.

Scientists have learned much about the general ways in which different conditions affect the growth of snowflakes. They have long known, for example, that at temperatures above 5°F (-15°C), the water droplets tend to form needle-like crystals rather than flat, lacy stars. Extreme cold tends to produce dendrites with sharper tips.

Now, with the help of computers, some scientists are starting to unravel the complex physical forces that determine *precisely* how snowflakes form. One computer program can take information on temperature, humidity, and other factors and produce a picture of the snowflake that would form in those conditions. But the calculations are so complex that it takes the machine eight hours.

Tiny changes in weather conditions can produce almost infinite variations in the shape of snowflakes. But mathematicians say it may not be true that no two snowflakes are ever exactly the same. There may be 18 million snowflakes in a cubic foot of snow, and snow has been falling for a couple of billion years. It's likely that, at some point, at least one snowflake formed that was just like one that had formed before. But it's still unlikely that you'll ever see two identical flakes at the same time.

Sometimes weather conditions make it impossible even to distinguish individual flakes. In warmer air, the crystals link together to form clumps of snow, sometimes up to an inch across. Such a clump may contain several thousand snowflakes.

And when snowflakes of any size reach the ground, they change their shape. Even if the crystals don't melt, evaporation and condensation reshape them into tiny smooth-sided granules within a very short time. The beautiful patterns disappear, taking the snowflakes' secrets with them.

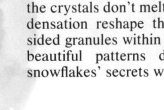

YOUNG PHOTOGRAPHERS

A photograph can be as striking and as haunting as a great painting or a fine poem. Today's young photographers know that, and they experiment to achieve the best results—with bold black-and-white patterns, hand-tinted colors, and other unusual effects.

The photographs on these pages were all winners in the 1987 Scholastic/Kodak Photo Awards program. The program offers scholarships and awards to junior and senior high school students in the United States. But besides the awards, the young photographers whose work is shown here had the satisfaction of producing beautiful pictures.

Crayons and Spruttle,
by Robbie Parker, 15,
Miami, Florida

Reflection by Hand, by Jimmy Hirabayashi, 17, Palos Verdes, California

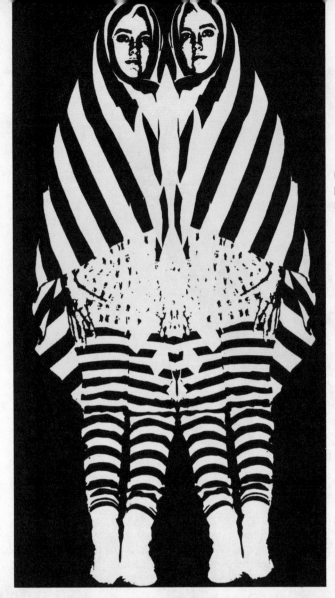

Untitled,
by Dylan Long, 17,
South Bend, Indiana

For Esme,
by Elizabeth Fox, 17,
Winter Garden, Florida

Untitled,
by Bryan Horne, 17,
Burbank, California

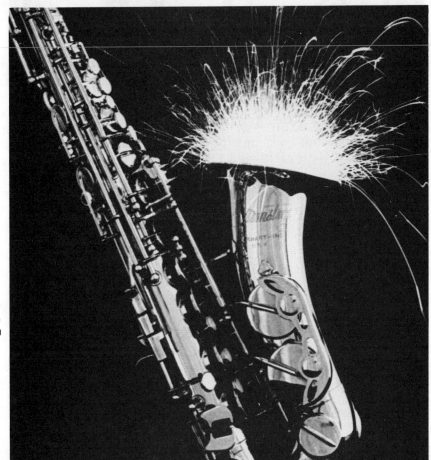

Sax,
by Ron Horn, 16,
Tucson, Arizona

Big Day For A Small Knight

In days of old when castles were new, there lived a band of brave knights who protected the beautiful Kingdom of St. Ives. Sir Bramwell the Brave was the most courageous of the knights. Sir Webster the Wise made the important decisions. Sir Quentin the Quick was the fastest, and Sir Val the Vain was the most handsome.

But there was one knight who was much smaller than the others, and he wasn't particularly good at anything. His name was Sir Percy. His fellow knights called him "Sir Percy the Puny" behind his back.

No matter how hard Sir Percy tried, he couldn't do anything right. But there was no harder working knight than Sir Percy, who wanted to be noticed. He wanted the King to invite him to a Royal Feast. And he wanted to sit next to the King's beautiful daughter, Princess Penelope.

But the King never invited the small knight to a feast, or lunch, or even breakfast! And Princess Penelope didn't even know that Sir Percy was alive. The only friend Percy had was an ordinary gray pigeon, whom he called Pip. The other knights laughed behind Percy's back.

"A common old pigeon! Not even a small hawk," said Sir Webster the Wise.

"Perhaps the King will dub him Sir Percy the Birdbrain!" laughed Sir Quentin the Quick.

"Maybe we should call the bird Pipsqueak —just like Sir Percy!" howled Sir Val the Vain.

But wherever Sir Percy went, Pip went too. "Don't worry," Sir Percy assured Pip. "Someday they'll notice us. And they won't laugh, either!"

"Squawk!" answered Pip.

One day, the local dragon decided it was time to stir up trouble in the peaceful town of St. Ives. So he frightened a milkmaid, who dropped two full buckets of milk and ran straight to the castle.

"Something must be done," said the King, after hearing her story. "Call for my knights!"

Sir Quentin the Quick arrived first. "I will be the first to hunt down the dragon," he promised.

Sir Bramwell the Brave arrived next. "I will face the dragon without fear," he vowed.

"I will discover a way to outsmart the dragon," said Sir Webster the Wise.

"And I will be the most handsome knight in the victory parade!" added Sir Val.

The four knights were ready to leave when they heard a soft voice. "Excuse me, but I would like to fight the dragon, too." The King and the knights turned around in great surprise. There stood Sir Percy and Pip!

"I will try my best to chase the dragon away from the village," answered Sir Percy.

"Squawk!" added Pip.

The knights roared with laughter. But the King, who was a good King after all, silenced them. "Very well, Sir Percy. You will join the royal hunt for the dragon. And I wish you the very best of luck."

And so the knights left in search of the dragon. He had left a trail of shriveled trees, burnt grass, and blackened bushes all around St. Ives. The trail ended at a large cave.

"This must be the home of the ferocious dragon," said Sir Webster, wisely.

"We'll rush in and surprise him!" said Sir Quentin, quickly.

"I'll be the first to go," bravely stated Sir Bramwell.

"And I'll—" began Sir Val.

"Squawk!" said Pip. The other knights turned to look at Sir Percy, whom they had forgotten, as usual.

"And what about you, Sir Pipsqueak . . . I mean, Sir Puny . . . I mean, Sir Pigeon?" asked Sir Val.

Sir Percy thought for a moment. "I will do whatever has to be done."

The other four knights howled with laughter until they heard a roar.

"The dragon! We must do something!" shouted Webster.

Sir Bramwell, being very brave, raised his shield and took a step toward the cave. Suddenly, flames leaped out at him, and his great shield melted into a little puddle.

Sir Webster tried to think of something clever to do. "Hurry, Sir Webster," urged Sir Quentin the Quick.

Just then the dragon poked his head out of the cave and roared a mighty roar. The knights all took ten steps backward. Pleased with the impression he had made, the dragon breathed fire. The knights all screamed and took ten more steps backward.

"Squawk!" cried Pip.

"Somebody do something!" urged Sir Val.

Then the dragon took two steps forward, breathing fire and roaring at the same time. The knights took ten more steps backward. And with the tenth step, they fell down into a huge pit. It was a trap the dragon had set for them.

"Our time has come," moaned Sir Val as they all waited for the dragon to attack.

But the dragon never did. He turned away and headed straight for St. Ives!

"We must warn the King!" cried Percy.

Sir Quentin and Sir Val were quick to point out that they could not possibly reach St. Ives before the dragon, who could run ten times faster than they could. Besides, Sir Webster still had to figure a way out of the pit.

Sir Percy wasn't listening. He was too busy writing on a piece of paper. Then he folded the paper and put it in Pip's beak. "Well, Pip, it's all up to you now."

The little pigeon flapped his wings and

soared out of the pit. He flew high above the dragon as he ran toward St. Ives. Pip flew straight to the King and dropped the note in his lap.

"What's this?" asked the King, reading the note. "A dragon? A mirror?" Then he thought a moment. "Call out my guards! We have work to do."

So as the dragon hurried toward St. Ives, the King prepared for his arrival. And when he reached the town, instead of seeing houses and shops, the dragon saw another ferocious, fire-breathing dragon—as big as he was! He took one look at the other dragon, turned tail, and ran—*away* from St. Ives!

It took the knights several hours to get out of the pit, and they didn't reach St. Ives until the end of the day. They were amazed to see a huge party going on. The center of attention was none other than Pip, the "common" pigeon. When the people saw Sir Percy, they cheered!

"But how—" mumbled Sir Bramwell.

"But why—" asked Sir Val.

"Sir Percy saved the day when he sent Pip to me," explained the happy King. "He told us the dragon was on his way. And he suggested that we take Sir Val the Vain's mirror —which is truly large—and stand it on the edge of town." The King chuckled. "I don't think that dragon will be back for at least a hundred years!"

"*My* mirror? Then *I* saved the day," said Sir Val, vainly.

The King shook his head. "No, Sir Val. This day belongs to Sir Percy and Pip. Without their cleverness, St. Ives would be no more. From now on, we'll call him Sir Percy the Proud!"

"Squawk!" said Pip.

The King invited Percy and Pip to a huge royal feast. Sir Percy was seated close to Princess Penelope, who now definitely knew who he was.

From that day on, the dragon never returned to St. Ives. And Sir Percy the Proud —along with Pip—spent many happy days with the good King and his beautiful daughter Penelope.

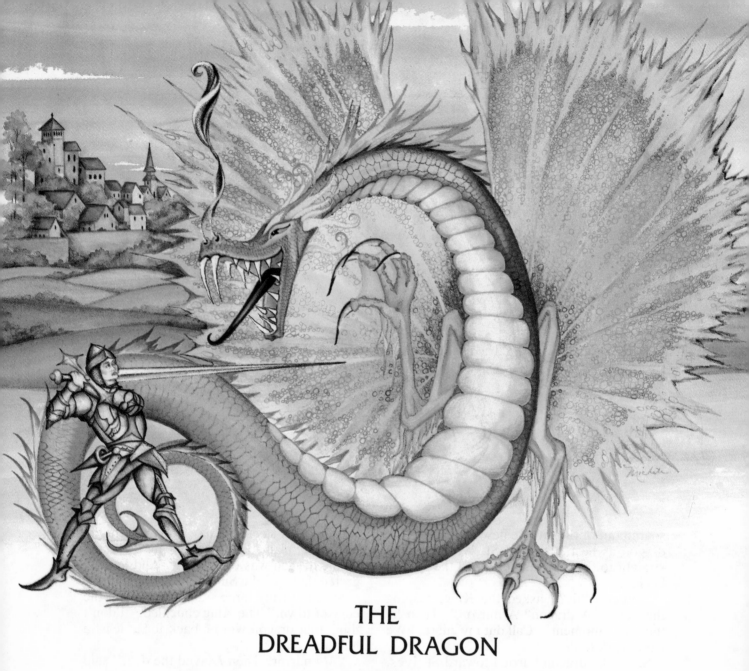

THE
DREADFUL DRAGON

Long, long ago, an old story tells, the people of a city in North Africa lived in terror of a menace outside their gates—an evil dragon. Each day the dragon appeared, demanding food. At first the people gave it sheep, but it soon demanded men and then young maidens.

To satisfy the dragon's horrid appetite, the king of the city ordered that all the young maidens draw lots each day to see who would be sacrificed. The lot finally fell to the king's own daughter. Sick at heart, he watched her walk through the city gates to face the waiting dragon.

Suddenly a strange knight appeared. Raising his sword, he spurred his horse at the dragon and battled it until the evil beast fell to the ground. Then he cut off its head.

The knight was George of Lydda, and the story is the famous tale of St. George and the dragon. In some versions, he marries the princess; in others, he rides off to do more good deeds. But St. George is only one of many heroes who have fought dragons through the pages of myth and legend.

Dragons appear in stories from nearly every part of the world. Some, like the dragon in the St. George tale, are evil. Others, especially in Chinese myths, are powerful but kind, even helpful. Stories of dragons are among the oldest in the world—some reach back nearly 4,000 years.

MYTHICAL MONSTERS

The stories agree on what a dragon is in general terms: a huge, scaly, lizardlike creature that can spit fire. But they differ on the specifics of dragon appearance.

Many dragons had batlike wings and could fly. Some had horns, sharp spines along their backs, and barbs on the ends of their tails. All had sharp fangs. Most dragons had legs and claws —two legs or four legs, like the legs of eagles or lions. But some were more like snakes: legless, wingless, or both.

Some dragons were said to live in wells or in deep forest pools. Other dragons were thought to live in swamps, rivers, and lakes; underground, in caves; or on high, inaccessible mountains. Dragons were believed to share a common love for jewels and other treasure. But while European dragons were heartless predators with insatiable appetites for human flesh, Chinese dragons were said to be content with an occasional bird.

The reason dragons varied so much is simple: They appear in many stories, but there is no evidence that they ever appeared on Earth. They are mythical creatures, so they take any form that the imagination gives them.

Some people have suggested that dragons represent a distant memory of dinosaurs. But dinosaurs died out long before humans appeared on Earth. Most dragons are something like certain living creatures—crocodiles, for example, or large lizards. On the island of Komodo in the Malay Archipelago, lizards called Komodo dragons grow up to 10 feet (3 meters) long. It's possible that the first dragon stories sprang up after people saw startling creatures like these.

The absence of real dragons hasn't prevented people from claiming to see them and even producing "specimens." Reports of dragon sightings were common in Europe through the 1600's, and preserved "dragon babies"—usually stitched together from lizard skins and bat wings—were sold. A few dragon sightings have even been reported in this century. But most people today accept the fact that dragons lived only in legend.

EARLY DRAGONS

Monsters of many kinds figured in the tales told by early peoples, especially in stories of the world's creation. Often it's unclear what these monsters were supposed to look like, but some are thought to have been dragons.

Another ancient tale arose in Babylonia, about 1800 B.C. It tells that at the dawn of the universe, the forces of evil and chaos were led by the dragonlike goddess Tiamat. The Babylonian sun god, Marduk, defeated her by using the wind as his ally. When the dragon opened her gaping jaws to devour him, he drove the wind into her mouth so that she couldn't close it. Then he shot an arrow down her throat to her heart (a dragon-slaying method used by many later heroes) and killed her.

The ancient Egyptians told of a huge serpent, Apophis, who was the enemy of their sun god, Re. Each night the sun god disappeared into the underworld to fight this monster. Each morning, having won the battle, he reappeared.

Our word "dragon" comes from the Greek word *drakon*, which was used to refer to any type of snake. Many Greek tales tell of heroes who defeated dragonlike monsters. The god Apollo, for example, slew the serpent monster Python. These tales are similar to stories about dragons that became popular in Europe during the Middle Ages. Like the later tales, they show the forces of good (represented by the hero) triumphing over evil (represented by the dragon).

DRAGONS OF EUROPE

The evil dragons of medieval Europe were always causing trouble. If a well went bad, the reason was doubtless that a dragon was living in it. If fire broke out in the middle of the night, dragons flying overhead had caused it with their fiery breath. Even when dragons didn't cause calamity, they were connected with it. Sightings of dragons were often reported just before catastrophic events such as invasions or outbreaks of plague. Dragons were pictured at the edges of early maps, marking the beginnings of dangerous, unknown lands.

Europeans believed there were several distinct types of dragons. The wyvern, for example, was a fierce, flying dragon that carried the plague. The amphiptère was a legless dragon that lived in Egypt and Arabia and guarded the trees that produced frankincense resin. The lindworm had no wings and was said to live in Central Asia, where Marco Polo claimed to have seen several. The guivre lacked legs as well as wings and was said to live in forests and wells. Most fantastic of all was the vouivre, a dragon that lived in the French Alps and was covered head to claw with jewels.

Besides these types, there were many famous individual dragons. One of the best known in Norse mythology is Fafnir, who began life as a giant. Fafnir killed his father to gain a hoard of gold and a magic ring that could make more gold. Then he changed into a dragon to guard his treasure better.

Fafnir ravaged the countryside until the hero Siegfried came along. Siegfried, like many other dragon-slayers, used brains as well as brawn to defeat his scaly foe. He dug a pit along a path the dragon used and waited in it. When the dragon came down the path and passed over him, he drove his sword into the monster's unprotected underside.

If the number of tales are any indication, Britain must once have fairly crawled with dragons. Among them was the Laidly Worm of Northumberland—a princess who was changed into a dragon by her wicked stepmother. Her brother returned from overseas, changed her back with a kiss, and turned the stepmother into a toad.

Another story tells how the heir of Lambton Hall went fishing one day and caught an odd-looking, fanged worm. Unthinkingly, he tossed it into a well on his way home. Years later the creature emerged from the dank well as a full-grown dragon and set about terrorizing the countryside. The young lord killed it with a clever plan: He wore spiked armor, so that when the dragon wrapped its coils around him it wounded itself.

Russians who listened to fireside tales knew that it was unwise to strike a bargain with a dragon. According to one tale, Gorynych, a dragon with several heads and even more tails, lived near Kiev. He was defeated in battle by Dobrynja Nikitich, who let him live on the condition that he stop destroying the countryside and carrying off young maidens. That, however, was what European dragons did best—so it wasn't long before Gorynych swooped down on Kiev and snatched a princess. Dobrynja galloped in pursuit to the dragon's lair, where he freed the princess and dispatched the monster once and for all.

CHINESE DRAGONS

The Chinese believed that dragons were powerful, magical, and friendly beings—not evil monsters to be slain. Dragons were honored and feared because their powers over the forces of nature were so great. By simply flying up into the sky, they could bring gentle rains to make crops grow. Chinese farmers would beat gongs to frighten the dragons into the air when they needed rain. But when dragons were angry, they caused floods, windstorms, and destruction.

Many Chinese scholars separated dragons into four types, each with its own job. The T'ien-lung, or Celestial Dragon, supported the palaces of the gods in heaven. The Shen-lung, or Spirit Dragon, governed wind and weather. It was said to be a lazy dragon that always tried to hide from work. The Ti-lung was the Dragon of the Earth, with power over rivers and streams. Every river was said to have its own dragon lord, who lived in a palace beneath the water. The fourth type was the Fu ts'ang-lung, or Dragon of Hidden Treasure, who guarded all the precious minerals underground.

Other writers classified dragons according to differences in their appearance. For example, the Imperial Dragon had five claws and was a symbol reserved for the emperor. Some dragons were thought to look like, and be related to, fish or horses. Nine dragons with different traits were believed to protect objects ranging from bells and swords to gates, bridges, and rooftops. Some tales told that dragons could assume human form and even shrink themselves to the size of mice.

Still other writers divided dragons by color. Blue dragons, for example, were considered omens of spring. Red and black dragons fought in the clouds and produced storms. Yellow dragons were the most honored, symbols of intelligence and virtue. But some people said that dragons could change color if they chose.

The Chinese believed that dragons hatched from huge, jewel-like eggs. These eggs lay near riverbanks for as long as 1,000 years before the young, snakelike creatures emerged. Newborn dragons immediately began to grow, taking 3,000 years to reach their final form. Along the way, they passed through various stages, sprouting scales, shaggy manes, claws, horns, and wings.

Parts of a dragon's body were thought to have strong medicinal powers. Chinese apothecaries sold powders that were said to be ground dragon's bone (for fevers and paralysis) or teeth (for madness and headache). Dragon blood was said to turn to amber when it touched the ground.

The Chinese believed that most important of all was a dragon's pearl, which it kept in its mouth or in the folds of skin under its

jaw. The pearl was said by some to symbolize wisdom and by others to stand for the sun, the moon, or life itself. But by all accounts, the pearl possessed great magic.

One Chinese story tells of a poor boy who finds a dragon's pearl lying in a field. He takes it back to the house where he lives with his widowed mother and puts it in the empty rice jar. In the morning, the jar is full. The boy and his mother find that the pearl will provide them not only with rice but with all the food they need, as well as silk and money. They keep it secret, and their wealth grows.

Soon the other people in the village grow jealous, and the headman goes to the boy's house to investigate. The boy hides the pearl by putting it into his mouth. But he swallows it by mistake—and is changed into a fire-breathing dragon.

In Chinese culture today, the dragon remains an important symbol, associated with prosperity and good luck. But few people would expect to find a dragon's pearl. If dragons ever existed, the days when they roamed the world are gone.

COUNTRY WOOD

Spring flowers, folk dolls, calico cats—capture the charm of the country with these delightful craft projects. Each uses ready-made wood cutouts that are available in craft stores, and you can buy hundreds of different kinds. They can be used to make clothes and key racks, wall plaques, table centerpieces, tree ornaments, even jewelry. It's a wonderful way to use your imagination and have a lot of fun at the same time.

Whichever project you decide on, certain basic supplies are needed: fine sandpaper, acrylic paints, paintbrushes, polyurethane or clear acrylic spray, and glue. If you're making an object that's meant to be hung on a wall, you'll need a sawtooth hanger and small nails with which to attach the hanger to the back of the object.

And no matter what the project, certain basic steps should be followed: First, sand each piece of wood until there are no rough edges. Then paint the pieces. After they dry, give them a second coat of paint. Sometimes you may decide to stain an object rather than paint it. This works well for baskets, boxes, plaques, and other background pieces onto which you'll glue the wood cutouts. Stained items don't need a second coat unless you want to give them a deeper color. Last, cover the painted or stained surfaces with several coats of polyurethane or acrylic spray. Let the pieces dry in-between coats. (Take care not to use polyurethane or acrylic on surfaces that will be glued together. These coatings tend to diminish glue's holding power.)

Now let's see how the objects shown here are made. The wood tulips pictured on the opposite page are placed in a mushroom basket that can be gotten at a supermarket. But any type of basket, box, or other container can be used. Paint the flowers and container in colors that will match the decor of the room in which the object will be placed. Glue thick layers of foamboard to the inside bottom of the container. Then embed the flower stems in the foamboard and secure them in place with glue. A layer of fine wood shavings called excelsior is used to cover the foamboard. Excelsior is a widely used packing material. It's also available in craft stores.

You can keep your room tidy with a peg rack like the one shown below. Paint the peg rack a bright color. If you wish, paint the pegs a different color than the background wood. Decide which wood cutouts you'd like to attach to the top of the rack—children, animals, a row of houses, a black silhouetted horse and

carriage. With a pencil, lightly draw designs on the cutouts (they can also be painted solid colors). When you paint the designs, make sure to let each color dry before you border it with a second color. When the paint is completely dry, glue the cutouts to the rack and use the polyurethane or acrylic spray.

For a whimsical touch, wrap a string of hearts around one of the pegs. Each of the hearts shown here actually consists of two wood cutouts—a large heart painted red and a small one painted pink. The small heart is glued to the center of the large heart. The string is glued to the backs of both large hearts.

A plaque holding a gaggle of geese or two smiling cats will steal your heart—or the heart of anyone you might give it to. Many different backgrounds can be used: fence designs (such as the ones shown here), squares, ovals, circles. Paint or stain the background. Then paint your country critters and a big red heart. Center these on the plaque and glue them in place. Cover with polyurethane or acrylic.

Basket lids are another popular background for country crafts.

BASKET - SIDE - VIEW

These are available in craft stores, but sometimes you can get them from supermarkets. They can be decorated in many different ways, using not only wood cutouts but also pinecones, dried flowers, colorful bows, and stuffed calico animals.

The basket lid shown here holds half a straw basket, made by cutting a lightweight basket in half. The half basket is attached to the stained lid by using glue from a hot glue gun. Bright green satin ribbons are woven through openings in the basket and held in place with glue. A matching bow is glued to the front. The basket is filled with white foam packing "peanuts." Excelsior or sphagnum moss can also be used. Three brightly painted tulips are set into the basket.

Basket lids can be edged with curved messages such as "Welcome," "Season's Greetings," or "I love country!" You can buy individual letters to create your message, or you can buy curved messages all ready for painting.

Try your hand at these fun crafts. You'll be delighted with the charm of country wood!

115

ROBOTS AND BEYOND

Robots and other "intelligent machines" can perform amazing feats. They play chess, draw pictures, help assemble cars, "speak," "hear," and "see." A typical industrial robotics system takes a minute and a half to complete a task that takes a human worker 30 to 40 minutes. Moreover, the system does the job with 98 percent accuracy, compared to 65 percent accuracy for the worker.

But are robots really as intelligent as people? Well, no robot is clever enough to tie a pair of shoelaces. Most of those that "speak" and "hear" use fewer words than the average 3-year-old child. Those that "see" have limited vision—one robot, specially equipped with two video-camera eyes, took more than an hour to cross a room while avoiding obstacles in its path.

Despite their limitations, however, robots are getting better all the time. Artificial intelligence—the art of making machines that perform tasks requiring intelligence—is an exciting field, one where new developments are occurring all the time. In 1987, this field became the subject of a special exhibit, "Robots and Beyond: The Age of Intelligent Machines." The exhibit opened at the Museum of Science in Boston and was scheduled to travel to seven other U.S. cities before closing in 1989.

The exhibit focused on four areas of artificial intelligence: robot senses (the ability to see, feel, and hear); robots in the workplace; expert systems (computers that act as experts in a given subject); and robots of the future.

Robot Senses. Vision remains one of the most difficult problems in artificial intelligence, and machines that can see as well as people have yet to be developed. But already existing are scanners that can read printed material and bar codes on the packages in supermarkets. The exhibit featured a machine that could read text aloud, in a computer synthesized voice, and one that could recognize simple objects like combs and keys.

Another demonstration showed how machines can be programmed to recognize objects using motion cues. Visitors walking up to one display could watch themselves on a video screen—but when they stopped moving, they disappeared. A companion display took the opposite tack: As long as visitors stood still, they could see themselves. When they moved, the image was scrambled.

Robots can also respond to the human voice. Such robots are used in some factories, and the exhibit had a device that allowed visitors to play a game by talking to a computer. Most robots that can "hear" have a vocabulary of just 100 to 1,000 words, but a few of the newest systems can recognize as many as 20,000 words. But recognizing words—written or spoken—isn't the same as understanding language or using it to form sentences that make sense. Computers and robots require extensive programming to understand even the simplest statements.

Another display at the exhibit demonstrated the sense of touch. Visitors who touched a patch of "skin" on this robot heard responses that ranged from "Oooh, I can feel that" to "Hey! Cut it out!" The "skin" was really piezoelectric film that changed pressure into electrical impulses.

Workers and Experts. Robots have made their greatest gains in the workplace, where they are taking over many monotonous and dangerous factory jobs. The exhibit offered insight into how robot workers do their jobs. One display showed how robot "muscles" are precisely controlled by computers and special motors. Others showed robots at work on an assembly line. And visitors could use a computer keyboard to control tiny robots working in a factory made of plastic building blocks.

Expert systems are computer programs that solve problems usually left to such experts as doctors, lawyers, geologists, and engineers. One such program, for example, takes information about land regions and forecasts what valuable minerals might be found there. Expert systems are stocked with information from living experts—not just facts, but hunches and rules of thumb that the real experts follow.

Several displays at the exhibit showed how expert systems work. One was a computerized game of three-dimensional tic-tac-toe. This machine had seven "experts" on tap, one for every aspect of the game. For example, one part of the program looked only for winning moves, and one looked for defensive moves. And another part of the program weighed the recommendations and decided among them.

Into the Future. Scientists estimate that, to be as intelligent as the human brain, a computer would have to be as big as the state of Texas and 100 stories tall. But machines are already making inroads into activities once considered for people only. The exhibit had a machine that could compose music in any style and one that could draw—not just mechanical drawings, but works of art. That raised a question: Were these machines creative, or were the true artists the people who programmed them?

The exhibit also showed how robots may help people in the future. Hero 2000—a mobile computer with sensors, a voice, and an arm—was on display. This robot is designed to be a home helper, and the day may come when every home has a similar device.

It was a robot, of course, that best summed up the exhibit. Jorel, a machine that mimicked human voice and movement, greeted visitors by announcing, "Humans, you are witnessing the beginning of a great new era."

Omnibot, a home robot of today, will most probably be replaced with more sophisticated "helpers" in the future.

117

HOORAY FOR HOLLYWOOD!

Hollywood: It's as much an idea as a place. It's Tinseltown, all glitter and no substance. It's the Dream Factory, spinning out fantasies that offer brief escape from the drabness of everyday life. It's the motion picture capital of the world, and few places have taken so strong a grip on so many imaginations. In 1987, the "place"—the city of Hollywood—celebrated the 100th anniversary of its founding in suitably brash style, with parties, parades, and other special events.

Hollywood's heyday belongs to the first half of this century. Much of the city's glitter has become tarnished in recent years, and few films are actually made there today. But some people believe that Hollywood—the city whose name has come to stand for all the glamour, past and present, of motion pictures—has begun to enjoy a revival. And the story of how the city and the motion picture industry grew up together is a part of American history.

A CITY IS BORN

A hundred years ago, Hollywood was just a tract of undeveloped land in Los Angeles County, California. A developer from Kansas, Harvey Wilcox, bought it and divided it into lots for resale in 1887. His wife named the subdivision Hollywood after the summer home of a friend—no holly trees grew on the land. To some, even the story of the name symbolizes the trait Hollywood has been most criticized for: artificiality.

Hollywood's early settlers were Midwesterners who outlawed theaters along with saloons. But in the early 1900's, the town began to change. The basic techniques of motion picture photography had been invented by Thomas Edison and others in the late 1800's, and by the turn of the century motion pictures were becoming popular entertainment. Most movies were made in New York City. But filmmakers soon began to move to the West Coast, seeking a better climate, cheap land and labor, and a variety of natural scenery.

In 1911, the Nestor Company built the first movie studio in Hollywood. Other filmmakers followed suit, among them D. W. Griffith and Thomas Ince. Jesse L. Lasky and Cecil B. De Mille made Hollywood's first feature-length film, *The Squaw Man,* a western. Films such as Griffith's *The Birth of a Nation* (1915), which chronicled the Civil War and Reconstruction eras, showed that movies could be epic productions. By 1920, filmmaking was one of the largest industries in the United States, and four out of five films were made in Hollywood.

The 1920's saw the film industry come to full flower. The major studios—Paramount, Fox, Metro-Goldwyn-Mayer, and others—had stables of stars under contract and shot their films on elaborate sets constructed on their enormous back lots. They ground out new feature films nearly every week and distributed them to their own theaters around the country.

Up to the mid-1920's, movies were silent. In theaters, a piano player would accompany a film. But then sound films were invented, and by the end of the decade "talkies" were shown everywhere. The Hollywood studios teetered on the edge of bankruptcy in the Great Depression of the 1930's, but the industry kept going: People went to the movies to forget their troubles. And in the mid-1930's, movies got a new boost from the use of color photography.

The films Hollywood produced were reflections of their times and of the dreams people held. In historical epics such as *Gone With the Wind* (1939), they re-created the past. In fantasies and fairy tales like *The Thief of Bagdad* (1924), they created times that never were. In wartime, Hollywood films promoted patriotism. In the hard times of the Great Depression, they glorified the struggles of ordinary people in films like *The Grapes of Wrath* (1940)—and showed how high-rollers and criminals lived in countless gangster films. In Westerns, comedies, and dramas of all kinds, they always entertained.

Each new film was met by eager fans. And as the film industry grew, so did Hollywood's glamorous image. The city of Los Angeles grew up around it, but Hollywood remained separate—and special.

THE HOLLYWOOD STARS

From the earliest days of Hollywood through its heyday in the 1930's and 1940's, it was the leading actors and actresses who captured the public's attention—both on screen and in their not-so-private lives. Fans kept up with the latest news of the stars by reading *Photoplay* and other movie magazines. And there was plenty to keep up with

—Hollywood quickly developed a reputation for fast living, excess, and scandal.

The studios were quick to realize that famous actors and actresses drew people to the movies. They scoured the world for talent, and they created the star system. Stars were "discovered" and promoted—sometimes with new names, capped teeth, dyed hair, and other changes. But the greatest movie stars had a natural on-screen appeal that couldn't be created.

Among the great stars of silent films were comedians such as Charlie Chaplin, who came to Hollywood from Britain and was best known for his "Little Tramp"character. Like Chaplin, most of the early stars played stock characters on screen. Canadian-born Mary Pickford, for example, usually appeared as a spunky small-town girl and became known as "America's Sweetheart."

Clara Bow was the "It" girl, the embodiment of the 1920's flapper. Douglas Fairbanks played swashbuckling adventurers, and Rudolph Valentino played smoldering Latin lovers. When Valentino died unexpectedly at the age of 31, thousands mourned his death.

Many stars of the silent era didn't make the transition to talkies—their voices weren't as appealing as their looks. Among those who did make the switch was Greta Garbo, the glamorous Swedish leading lady who brought a sense of mystery to the screen. And new stars came to Hollywood with the era of sound films. Will Rogers drew audiences with his homespun cowboy humor. Clark Gable's rough-edged appeal made him a top leading man of the 1930's, along with Cary Grant, Jimmy Stewart, and Gary Cooper. Joan Crawford, Carole Lombard,

Bette Davis—there was no lack of leading ladies either. But perhaps the biggest star of the 1930's was a child: Shirley Temple.

In each decade new Hollywood stars emerged—among them Humphrey Bogart, Gregory Peck, Spencer Tracy, and Katharine Hepburn in the 1940's; James Dean, John Wayne, Marilyn Monroe, and Audrey Hepburn in the 1950's; Elizabeth Taylor, Doris Day, Rock Hudson, and Paul Newman in the 1960's. In most cases, their careers continued for many years.

The studios paid their stars fabulous salaries and guarded their images, sometimes even choosing the clothes they wore offscreen. Hollywood stars set fashion trends in clothing, hairstyles, and makeup. Their footprints and handprints were immortalized in wet cement on the sidewalk outside Grauman's (now Mann's) Chinese Theater. People gossiped about their marriages (and divorces) and sighed over their luxurious Hollywood homes. And young people everywhere dreamed of becoming glamorous movie stars. Many went to Hollywood, in the hope of being "discovered" or of just catching a glimpse of their favorites outside the Brown Derby restaurant and other haunts of the stars.

BEHIND THE SCENES

As important as the stars were, however, they never could have appeared on screen without the efforts of many other people. Making a film, now as in Hollywood's early days, is a team effort, involving everyone from directors and producers down to wardrobe and lighting assistants.

The process begins with a script put together by one or more screenwriters. Pro-

ducers figure out a budget for the film, and actors and actresses are cast for the main roles. Then set designers and costume designers go to work. If the film is to be shot on location—that is, away from the studio—production teams go out looking for suitable filming sites.

But often exotic locations are re-created at the studio, using constructed sets, painted backdrops, and other tricks. A shot of a ship at sea, for example, might be set up using a model boat in a tank of water. In the 1923 epic *The Ten Commandments,* the parting of the Red Sea was simulated with blocks of quivering gelatin. Today such special effects are created with computers and other high-tech tools. They have become increasingly important and sophisticated in the science fiction films of recent years.

Once the sets and costumes are ready, filming can begin. Filming may take weeks or months, and scenes are shot in the most convenient order—not in the order in which they'll appear in the film. Each day, the director reviews the day's shots, or rushes, and selects the best ones.

When the shooting is over, the reels of film are edited. Scenes are put in the correct order, and the movie is trimmed to an appropriate length. A background musical score is added, along with background sounds like train whistles and engines. Finally, the film is ready for distribution.

In Hollywood's heyday, the opening of a major new film was a celebrity event. Fans, photographers, and reporters lined up outside premiere theaters in Hollywood or New York to watch the stars, decked out in evening dress, arrive in limousines to view the film. Today such grand openings are still held, but they seldom attract so much attention. That's just one of the changes that have come to Hollywood in recent times.

END OF AN ERA

The seeds of Hollywood's decline were planted in the late 1940's. Rising labor costs and strikes increased the studios' expenses. They were charged with violating antitrust laws and ordered to sell off their theaters to independent operators. Then television arrived on the scene, and sales of movie tickets fell. People could stay home and be entertained in their living rooms. New film tech-

niques—wide-screen CinemaScope and 3-D movies—and ever more spectacular films failed to win the customers back.

These events brought many changes to the movie industry. Producers found that it was often more economical to make films abroad, where labor costs were lower. Even so, the studios became more cautious and cost conscious about their films. Many studios were taken over by large business conglomerates and branched out into television and recording. Today the film studios mainly finance and distribute films made by independent producers, rather than producing their own. The average film now costs about $14 million to produce.

Only one major studio, Paramount, is still located in Hollywood, and many back lots have been converted to office space. As the studios left, so did the stars, moving on to posh homes in Beverly Hills and the Los Angeles suburbs. Stores and other businesses closed, street crime increased, and the once-glamorous Hollywood streets took on a tawdry air.

In recent years the movie industry has faced a new challenge: the home video, which makes movies available to anyone who has a video player. But the industry has also seen a revival. New directors and producers have scored successes with films directed toward younger audiences. And new stars have appeared.

Most people agree that the film stars of today are different from those of the 1940's. Few command the degree of public attention that the earlier stars received. Nor are they eager to be typecast—they're more interested in showing their versatility as actors by playing a variety of roles. Most are more independent and less closely tied to the studios, and some are producers and directors in their own right. But their new faces have helped revitalize the movie industry.

With the revival of the film industry has come the beginning of a revival of Hollywood. People have begun to restore some of the city's famous buildings. Some filmmakers have returned, and groups such as the Screen Actors Guild have been persuaded to keep their headquarters in town. As Hollywood marked its 100th anniversary, it had good reason to celebrate its future as well as its past.

HOLLYWOOD: LEGEND AND REALITY

As Hollywood celebrated its 100th birthday, a special exhibit called "Hollywood: Legend and Reality" was midway through a two-year tour of six U.S. cities. The exhibit, organized by the Smithsonian Institution, explored the development of the motion picture industry and its impact on American culture.

On display were many items that recalled Holly-wood's golden era and gave glimpses behind the scenes of some famous films. Among them were props, such as the piano that was the centerpiece of Rick's Café in the film *Casablanca* (upper left), and costume sketches, such as Cecil Beaton's sketch for the costume Audrey Hepburn wore as the cockney flower seller in *My Fair Lady* (upper right). Also in the exhibit were a neon theater sign (lower left), from the days when major studios owned their own chains of movie theaters, and a matte painting (lower right) used in the filming of *The Wizard of Oz*. The painting allowed filmmakers to create the illusion of the Emerald City without actually building a set.

INDEX

ILLUSTRATION CREDITS
AND ACKNOWLEDGMENTS